Eph.B.Lewy.

2/9/24.

SAYINGS AND PORTRAITS
OF
JOHN WESLEY

THE ROMNEY PORTRAIT OF WESLEY.
(Reproduced from a Baxter print.)

Sayings and Portraits

OF

JOHN WESLEY

Compiled and edited by
JOHN TELFORD, B.A.

London

THE EPWORTH PRESS

J. ALFRED SHARP

First Edition, 1924.

920
w. 5 1 3 S a

MADE AND PRINTED IN GREAT BRITAIN.

PREFACE

THIS little volume will bring its readers into intimate contact with John Wesley. Its portrait gallery, which is peculiarly rich, specially for the later years, shows in what high regard he was held. The portraits represent him at many stages in his pilgrimage from manhood to venerable old age. Such a collection of Wesley portraits has never before been published, and the notes opposite each give interesting details as to the artists to whom we owe them, and the circumstances under which they were produced. We get still closer to Wesley in the quotations from his letters and his various works. The arrangement followed is twofold. There is a word for every day of a year which may serve as a motto or a seed thought for busy men and women. This is followed by more extended quotations, which give his doctrinal position, his views as to dress, education, and many other subjects. They trace the various stages of his own work and of that of Whitefield, Fletcher, and other fellow labourers. We thus look into the heart of the man; discern his motives, and understand the way in which Providence used him as the Evangelist of England and the inspirer of new views of Christian life and service. So far as possible the source of every quotation is given from the octavo edition of the *Works* (1829-31) fourteen volumes (5th edition, 1860), and this it is felt will be appreciated by all workers in this field. The editor's father often told him how John Wesley met the class in Carlisle of which his grandfather was one of the first members. Wesley listened to their experience, and then gave them a charge which never ceased to sound in their ears: 'Now there are twelve of you, and all professing to have your hearts on fire with the love of God; if you are faithful, you are enough to set this city on fire.' Then he himself took fire, and added, 'Not this city only but this country, yea, the whole world.' Wesley was a mighty force in his own century, but his influence to-day is vaster and more widely extended than ever, and at that no one will wonder who feels in his own words the spirituality, the zeal, and the wisdom which marked everything that he said and did.

PREFACE

We owe various particulars as to the Wesley portraits to the notes by Mr. J. G. Wright in the *Proceedings* of the Wesley Historical Society, volumes iii and iv. Any information as to the present holders of the original paintings that still remain unlocated would be welcomed.

Special thanks are due to the Rev. John T. Waddy, B.A., whose careful study of the subject has enriched the collection and supplied the source of some quotations, and to others who have been keenly interested in the preparation of a volume which we hope will do its part in furthering those objects for which Wesley lived and laboured with never-flagging zeal and devotion.

JOHN TELFORD.

CONTENTS

A DAILY WORD FROM WESLEY

Hear ye, O hear! that ceaseless-pleading voice,
Which storm, nor suffering, nor age could still—
Chief prophet-voice through nigh a century's span!
Now silvery as Zion's dove that mourns,
Now quelling as the Archangel's judgement-trump,
And ever with a sound like that of old
Which, in the desert, shook the wandering tribes,
Or, round about storied Jerusalem,
Or by Gennesaret, or Jordan, spake
The words of life.

—R. W. GILDER.

JANUARY

1. I look upon all the world as my parish; thus far I mean, that in whatever part of it I am, I judge it meet, right, and my bounden duty to declare unto all that are willing to hear the glad tidings of salvation.

Journal, 11/6/39.

2. Leisure and I have taken leave of one another. I propose to be busy as long as I live, if my health is so long indulged me.

Works, xii. 20.

3. I thank you, I will think of it.

First saying as a child.

4. This love we believe to be the medicine of life, the never-failing remedy for all the evils of a disordered world, for all the miseries and vices of man.

Earnest Appeal, sect. 3.

5. Who would wish to live for any meaner purpose than to serve God in our generation?

Letter, 10/1/83.

6. Go on, for God is with you.

Letter, 22/10/76.

7. If ever I should listen to that siren song, 'Spare thyself,' I believe my Master would spare me no longer, but soon take me away.

Letter, 10/1/83.

8. You look inward too much, and upward too little.

Letter, 16/2/71.

9. You have your hands full of business, but it will not hurt you while your heart is free.

Letter, 5/1/83.

10. You are in God's school, and He will teach you one lesson after another till you have learned all His holy and acceptable will.

Letter, 1/4/84.

11. God can do His work by pleasure as well as by pain.

Letter, 1/4/84.

12. Whatever clouds may interpose between, His banner over you is love.

Letter, 28/3/85.

13. If we see God in all things, and do all for Him, then all things are easy.

Letter, 28/5/57.

14. While you help others, God will help you.

Letter, 31/8/84.

15. It will be given you without money and without price; you know not how soon.

Letter, 1783, to Mr. Orchard.

16. It is a great thing to seize and improve the very now.

Letter, 1/9/71.

17. Do all you can for so good a Master.

Letter, 31/7/84.

18. As long as you feel your own weakness and helplessness, you will find help from above.

Letter, 15/10/85.

19. I see God sitting upon His throne, and ruling all things well.

Letter, 31/8/55.

20. I must declare just what I find in the Book.

Journal, 2/11/72.

21. If he has bad tempers, he is no more a good man than the devil is a good angel.

Journal, 16/5/84.

22. A calm, even spirit goes through rough work far better than a furious one.

Journal, 23/6/66.

23. I love truth wherever I find it.

Letter, 13/10/62.

24. What is as clear to me as the sun at noonday is not so clear to every one.

Works, xiii. 289.

25. I am sick of opinions; I am weary to bear them. Give me solid and substantial religion; give me an humble, gentle lover of God and man.

Works, viii. 244.

26. Love supplies all the essentials of good breeding, without the help of a dancing-master.

Journal, 4/9/76.

27. Redeem the time, catch the golden moments as they fly.

Letter, 26/9/84.

28. I would do just as I do now—all the good I can while I live.

Journal, 26/10/71.

29. This world never made any one happy; and it is certain it never will. But God will.

Letter, 5/7/83.

30. Your calling is not only to do good, but to do all the good you possibly can.

Letter, 27/10/84.

31. If you would please men, please God.

Works, vii. 146.

FEBRUARY

1. All is good which lies in the way to glory.

   Journal, 29/8/57.

2. As long as we insist on the marrow of religion, Christ reigning in the heart, He will certainly prosper our labours.

   Letter, 18/1/86.

3. It is safer to think too little than too much of yourself.

   Letter, 30/10/85.

4. Be fruitful therefore in every good work, and God shall see very soon His whole image.

   Letter, 26/11/85.

5. By the grace of God I never fret; I repine at nothing; I am discontented with nothing. And to have persons at my ear fretting and murmuring at everything, is like tearing the flesh off my bones.

   Letter, 31/8/55.

6. *Vive hodie!* (Live to-day).

   Letter, 21/9/60.

7. It is the glory of the people called Metho-

dists that they condemn none for their opinions or modes of worship.

Letter, 3/10/83.

8. They think and let think, and insist upon nothing but Faith working by Love.

Letter, 3/10/83; cf. Works, vii. 315.

9. About eleven it came into my mind that this was the very day and hour in which I was taken out of the flames. I stopped and gave a short account of that wonderful Providence.

Journal, 9/2/50.

10. What is the real value of a thing but the price it will bear in eternity?

Letter, 30/11/70.

11. Do what in you lies, and He will do the rest.

Letter, 14/12/85.

12. You have need continually to be as a little child, simply looking up for whatever you want.

Letter, 21/12/76.

13. This religion we long to see established in the world, a religion of love, and joy, and peace.

Earnest Appeal, sect. 4.

14. Disappoint those who wait for your halting.

Letter, 5/9/85.

15. Duty is all I consider. Trouble and reproach I value not.

Letter, 6/5/74.

16. You cannot live on what God did yester-
day. Therefore He comes to-day.

Letter, 11/11/60.

17. Give Him your heart and it sufficeth.

Letter, 21/12/76.

18. O what mischief may be done by one
who means well!

Journal 12/10/60.

19. Though I am always in haste, I am never
in a hurry.

Letter, 10/12/77.

20. Do a little at a time that you may do
more.

Letter, 19/2/91.

21. Be diligent. Never be unemployed, never
be triflingly employed.

Twelve Rules of a Helper.

22. I do only one thing at a time, and I
do it with all my might.

Reynolds' *Anecdotes of Wesley,* p. 42.

23. I did my best; if I did wrong, it was
not the error of my will, but of my
judgement.

Works, xiii. 249.

24. While we live let us work our Lord's
work betimes; and in His time He will
give us our full reward.

Letter, 3/2/90.

25. God grant I may never live to be use-
less!

Journal, 28/6/83.

26. Our comfort is, He that made the heart can heal the heart.

Letter, 14/2/86.

27. How necessary for every one to be on the right foundation! We must be justified by faith, and then go on to sanctification.

Deathbed Saying.

28. There is no way into the holiest but by the blood of Jesus.

Deathbed Saying.

29. Whatever enemies you have, it is enough that you have a Friend who is mightier than them all. O let Him reign in your heart alone!

Letter, 14/6/57.

MARCH

1. The best of all is, God is with us!
   Deathbed Saying.

2. The world may not like our Methodists
   and Evangelical people, but the world
   cannot deny that they die well.
   Lecky, *England,* iii. 150.

3. Religion has nothing sour, austere, un-
   sociable, unfriendly in it; but, on the
   contrary, implies the most winning sweet-
   ness, the most amiable softness and
   gentleness.
   Works, xii. 47; *Letter,* 29/3/37.

4. I love that word, 'And Ishmael died in
   the presence of all his brethren.'
   Letter, 16/3/83.

5. Your help stands in Him alone. He will
   command all these things to work
   together for good.
   Letter, 14/2/86.

6. It is not safe to live or die without love.
   Letter, 10/8/75.

7. If you could take one advice, it would
   have a surprising effect. It is this, 'Take
   no thought for the morrow.'
   Letter, 26/2/78.

8. To-day only is yours. Look up, and He will bless you all to-day.
Letter, 26/2/78.

9. I go calmly and quietly on my way doing what I conceive to be the will of God.
Letter, 21/2/86.

10. I long to have you more and more deeply penetrated by humble, gentle, patient love.
Letter, 25/10/72.

11. Believe me you can find nothing higher than this (love), till mortality is swallowed up of life.
Letter, 25/10/72.

12. How shall we conquer if we do not fight?
Letter, 21/2/86.

13. Spend and be spent for a good Master.
Letter, 9/12/71.

14. Be equally ready to do and to suffer His whole will; and aspire after all His promises.
Letter, 5/3/78.

15. When our mind is hurried, it is hardly possible to retain either the spirit of prayer or of thankfulness.
Works, xii. 171; *Letter, 14/7/48.*

16. I am ashamed of my indolence and inactivity.
Letter, 25/3/74.

17. It is right to know ourselves, but not to

stop there. This is only of use if it leads us to know Him that loves and saves sinners.

Letter, 2/4/78.

18. One great office of prayer is to increase our desire of the things we ask for.

Notes on New Testament, Matt. vi. 8.

19. It is enough that Christ is yours: and He is wiser and stronger than all the powers of hell. Hang upon Him, and you are safe: lean on Him with the whole weight of your soul.

Works, xii. 371; *Letter,* 13/7/68.

20. Hang upon Him that loves you as a little child, living *to-day,* and trusting Him for *to-morrow.*

Letter, 1/1/70.

21. It is plain God sees it best for you frequently to walk in a thorny path.

Letter, 25/9/57.

22. I see abundantly more than I feel. I want to feel more love and zeal for God.

Letter, 24/2/86.

23. How many proofs must we have that there is no petition too little, any more than too great, for God to grant?

Journal, 27/4/55.

24. In every place we find working men most susceptible to religion.

Journal, 25/3/85.

25. All haughtiness, whether of heart, speech, or behaviour, vanishes away where love prevails.

Works, vii. 497.

26. I will not buy a cross, though I can bear it.

Letter, 15/1/70.

27. This will endear and sweeten every cross, which is only a painful means of a closer union with Him.

Letter, 1/1/70.

28. Meantime, bear your cross, and it will bear you. Seek an inward, not an outward, change.

Letter, 26/1/74.

29. Go on to universal self-denial, to temperance in all things, to a firm resolution of taking up daily every cross whereto you are called.

Works, vii. 75.

30. Nothing in the Christian system is of greater consequence than the doctrine of Atonement.

Letter, 7/2/78.

31. Money never stays with me: it would burn if it did. I throw it out of my hands as soon as possible, lest it should find a way into my heart.

Letter, 6/10/46.

APRIL

1. Can anything but love beget love?

   Works, vi. 175.

2. I submitted to be more vile, and proclaimed in the highways the glad tidings of salvation.

   Journal, 2/4/39.

3. God says to you as well as to me, 'Do all thou canst, be it more or less, to save the souls for whom My Son has died.'

   Letter, 25/3/74.

4. I seek two things in this world—truth and love. Whoever assists me in this search is a friend indeed, whether known or unknown to [me].

   Letter, 28/6/55.

5. O praise God for all you have; and trust Him for all you want!

   Letter, 11/7/78.

6. I take nothing ill that is meant well.

   Letter, 7/3/80.

7. I must act by my own conscience, not yours. And I really have a conscience.

   Letter, 7/3/80.

8. Be zealous and active for a good Master, and you will see the fruit of your labour.

Letter, 11/1/75.

9. I do not wonder that all the trials you feel do not interrupt the peace of God. They never need.

Letter, 14/1/80.

10. His grace is sufficient to keep you in, and to deliver you out of, all temptations.

Letter, 14/1/80.

11. Do not reason, but believe.

Letter, 1780, to Mrs. Rose.

12. Hang upon Him as a little child, and your eyes shall see the full salvation.

Do., 1780.

13. Trials are only blessings in disguise.

Letter, 24/7/80.

14. He prepares occasions of fighting, that you may conquer.

Letter, 6/5/74.

15. It is a great step toward Christian resignation, to be thoroughly convinced of that great truth, that there is no such thing as Chance in the world.

Letter, 2/1/81.

16. The more labour, the more blessing.

Letter, 16/3/76.

17. Sufferings are the gift of God to you. And they are all intended for your profit,

that you may be a partaker of His holiness.

Letter, 26/2/80.

18. Fortune is only another name for Providence, only it is *covered* Providence.

Letter, 2/1/81.

19. You and I are bigots to the Bible. We think the Bible language is like Goliath's sword: that 'There is none like it.'

Letter, 25/3/72.

20. Only take care to improve the Sabbaths, and He will stand every day at your right hand.

Letter, 22/10/80.

21. As it was evidently the providence of God which placed you in your present situation, He will doubtless give you grace sufficient for it.

Letter, 22/10/80.

22. There is but one thing to do, let us live and die unto Him that died for us.

Letter, 3/3/76.

23. You have need to be all alive yourselves, if you would impart life to others.

Letter, 3/12/80.

24. Be punctual. Whenever I am to go to a place the first thing I do is to get ready; then, what time remains is my own.

To his nephew Samuel,
Telford's ' John Wesley,' p. 355.

25. The more exercise he uses, winter or summer, the more health he will have.
Letter, 16/1/81.

26. The cheerfulness of faith you should aim at in and above all things.
Letter, 18/9/80.

27. You must not set the great blessing afar off, because you find much war within.
Letter, 18/9/80.

28. When I devoted to God my ease, my time, my fortune, my life, I did not except my reputation.
Life of Charles Wesley, ii. 283.

29. Look up, and expect Him that is mighty to save.
Letter, 18/11/80.

30. You have not such another flower in all your gardens.
(Of Nancy Bolton.) *Letter,* 11/1/75.

MAY

1. We are debtors to all the world. We are called to warn every one, to exhort every one, if by any means we may save some.
Letter, 11/12/72.

2. Little things contrary to our wills may be great blessings.
Letter, 2/12/78.

3. We have need to apply the general word, 'Take up thy cross, and follow Me,' to a thousand little particulars.
Letter, 2/12/78.

4. A smoky room, a cold morning, a rainy day, the dullness or perverseness of those we are with: these, and innumerable little crosses, will help us onward to the Kingdom.
Letter, 2/12/78.

5. Remember! you will be rewarded according to your *labour,* not according to your success.
Letter, 26/8/79.

6. Let us work while the day is.
Letter, 7/3/79.

7. I hope you will always be diligent in business as one branch of the business of Life.
Letter, 3/8/78.

27

8. What a blessing it is to have One Friend! How many have never found one in their lives!

Letter, 15/5/79.

9. If you need no book but the Bible, you are got above St. Paul. He wanted others too.

Large Minutes, 1770, Q.32.

10. Read the most useful books, and that regularly and constantly.

Large Minutes, 1770, Q.32.

11. I have often repented of judging too severely, but very seldom of being too merciful.

Letter, 20/10/87.

12. You are all, I hope, pressing on to the mark! See! the prize is before you!

Letter, 19/2/79.

13. Expect from Him, not what you deserve, but what you want—health of soul and health of body.

Letter, 16/8/78.

14. Find preachers of David Brainerd's spirit, and nothing can stand before them.

Journal, August 8, 1767.

15. Exhort all the believers, strongly and explicitly, to go on to perfection; and to expect every blessing God has promised, not to-morrow, but to-day!

Letter, 7/3/79.

16. Thou poor sinner, stay not to be any better, but take Him just as you are! Trust Him, praise Him now, the Lord will take you with His sweet force.
Letter, 29/11/74.

17. The more labour, the more blessing.
Letter, 9/10/79.

18. Work your work betimes; and in His time He will give you a full reward.
Letter, 1/11/78.

19. Loyalty is with me an essential branch of religion.
Letter, 25/6/77.

20. I received the surprising news that my brother had found rest to his soul. His bodily strength also returned from that hour. 'Who is so great a God as our God?'
Journal, 19/5/38.

21. Whenever the Holy Ghost teaches, there is no delay in learning.
Works, vii. 32.

22. Look up, and wait for happy days!
Letter, 26/10/78.

23. Cleave to Him with your whole heart, and you will have more and more reason to praise Him.
Letter, 13/11/78.

24. I felt my heart strangely warmed. I felt I did trust in Christ, Christ alone, for salvation; and an assurance was given me, that He had taken away *my* sins, even *mine*.
Journal, 24/5/38.

25. The moment I awaked, 'Jesus, Master,' was in my heart, and in my mouth; and I found all my strength lay in keeping my eye fixed upon Him, and my soul waiting on Him continually.

Journal, 25/5/38.

26. Beware of lukewarmness. Beware of cleaving to the present world. Let your treasure and your heart be above.

Letter, 27/11/83.

27. The knowledge of the Three-One-God is interwoven with all true Christian faith; with all vital religion.

Sermon LV., 7.

28. Still I insist, the *fact* (of the Trinity) you believe, you cannot deny; but the *manner* you cannot comprehend.

Sermon LV., 7.

29. If you have two or three that are strong in faith, they will wrestle with God in mighty prayer, and bring down a blessing on all that are round about them.

Letter, 11/2/79.

30. Chance has no share in the government of the world.

Letter, 11/2/79.

31. The Lord reigneth and disposes all things, strongly and sweetly, for the good of them that love Him.

Letter, 11/2/79.

JUNE

1. When we are justified, He gives us one talent; to those who use this He gives more. When we are sanctified, He gives as it were five talents.

   Letter, 3/6/74.

2. And if you use the whole power which is then given, He will not only continue that power, but increase it day by day.

   Letter, 3/6/74.

3. I care not for labour, but I want time.

   Letter, 23/10/79.

4. Walk in the narrowest path of the narrow way, and the Spirit of Glory and of Christ shall rest upon you.

   Letter, 12/8/74.

5. Stir yourself up before the Lord! Pray that you may be all alive.

   Letter, 10/8/79.

6. Labour to be serious, earnest, edifying in your daily conversations.

   Letter, 10/8/79.

7. There is a reward for bearing as well as doing His will.

   Letter, 2/3/73.

8. It is a mere groundless imagination that I love persons less for their plain dealing.

Letter, 1/11/79.

9. You are no more at liberty to throw away your health than to throw away your life.

Letter, 13/7/74.

10. Do as much to-day as you can do without hurting yourself, or disabling you from doing the same to-morrow.

Works, iv. 232 (1771 Ed.).

11. The way to heaven is singularity all over. If you move but one step towards God, you are not as other men are.

Sermon XXVI., §4.

12. I love the poor: in many of them I find pure genuine grace, unmixed with paint, folly, and affectation.

Letter, 25/9/57.

13. I frequently find a want of more light; but I want heat more than light.

Letter, 3/5/77.

14. The doing all which religion requires will not lessen, but immensely increase, our happiness.

Works, vi. 500.

15. This is the work which I know God has called me to; and sure I am that His blessing attends it.

Journal, 11/6/39 *(letter to Hervey).*

16. You work for a generous Master. Fight on and conquer all.
Works, xii. 395; *Letter*, 16/12/72.

17. O what a deal of work has our Lord to do here on earth! And may we be workers together with Him!
Letter, 13/5/74.

18. O John, pray for an advisable and teachable temper.
Letter, 28/7/75.

19. Dost thou love and serve God? It is enough. I give thee the right hand of fellowship.
Works, viii. 347.

20. There are two general ways wherein it pleases God to lead His children to perfection: Doing and Suffering. And let Him take one or the other, we are assured His way is best.
Letter, 17/2/74.

21. Be simple! Be a little child before God. Read and pray much.

22. See that every house is supplied with books.

23. It is not possible to avoid all pleasure even of sense, without the destroying the body; neither doth God require it at our hands.
Works, xi. 461.

24. Still be ready to do and to suffer the whole will of God.
Letter, 21/1/77.

3

25. Beware of indulging gloomy thoughts:
they are the bane of thoughtfulness.

Letter, 26/4/77.

26. You are encompassed with ten thousand
mercies; let these sink you into humble
thankfulness.

Letter, 26/4/77.

27. Nothing but the mighty power of God
can enable him [John Howard] to go
through his difficult and dangerous em-
ployments. But what can hurt us, if
God is on our side?

Journal, 28/6/87.

28. I entered into my eightieth year; but,
blessed be God, my time is not 'labour
and sorrow.' I find no more pain or
bodily infirmities than at five-and-twenty.

Journal, 28/6/82.

29. Keep at the utmost distance from foolish
desires, from desiring any happiness but
in God.

Works, xi. 462.

30. How soon may you hear 'the voice that
speaks Jehovah near!' Why shall it not
be to-day?

Letter, 26/1/74.

JULY

1. How amiable is courtesy joined to sincerity!
   Wesley Studies, p. 203.

2. You like to be honoured, but had you
   not rather be beloved?
   Works, vii. 146.

3. You may live in and to Jesus; yea, and
   that continually, by simple faith, and
   holy, humble love.
   Letter, 12/8/69.

4. It is a rule with me to take nothing ill
   that is well meant.
   Letter, 25/9/57.

5. The righteousness of Christ is necessary
   to *entitle* us to heaven, personal holiness
   to *qualify* us for it.
   Works, vii. 314.

6. The poor are the Christians. Let us take
   care to lay up our treasure in heaven.
   Letter, 30/9/86.

7. A little fatigue I do not regard, but I
   cannot afford to lose time.
   Letter, 17/2/76.

8. If He sees, and when He sees best, He
   will put more talents into your hands.
   Letter, 1/8/86.

9. In the meantime it is your wisdom to make the full use of those which you have.

Letter, 1/8/86.

10. Believing is the act of man, but it is the gift of God.

Letter, 7 Jan. (?) 1787 (to T. Lessey).

11. If we could once bring all our preachers, itinerant and local, uniformly and steadily to insist on those two points, Christ dying for us, and Christ reigning in us, we should shake the trembling gates of hell.

Letter, 28/12/74.

12. However tempted thereto by profit or pleasure, contract no intimacy with worldly-minded men.

Works, vi. 463.

13. Oh let no man think his labour of love is lost because the fruit does not immediately appear.

Journal, 13/6/42.

14. Every believer ought to *enjoy* life.

Letter, 27/7/87.

15. We cannot impute too much to divine Providence, unless we make it interfere with our free agency.

Letter, 26/4/77.

16. Keep your rules, and they will keep you.

Letter, 9/11/87.

17. God keeps you long in this school that you may thoroughly learn to be meek and lowly in heart, and to seek all your happiness in God.

Letter, 27/1/76.

18. Do not affect the gentleman. A preacher of the gospel is the servant of all.

Twelve Rules.

19. Never deny, never conceal, never speak doubtfully of what God hath wrought.

Letter, 12/11/76.

20. Keep to the whole Methodist discipline whoever is pleased or displeased.

Letter, 29/4/76.

21. Leave that with Him. The success is His. The work only is yours. Your point is this—work your work betimes; and in His time He will give you a full reward.

Letter, 4/11/74.

22. Envy will invent a thousand things, and with the most plausible circumstances.

Letter, 9/11/87.

23. Blessed be God, I do not slack my labour; I can preach and write still.

Journal, 1/1/90.

24. See that you be not ashamed of a good Master, nor of the least of His servants.

Letter, 18/1/76.

25. With what is past, or what is to come, we have little to do. *Now* is the day of Salvation.
    Letter, 21/4/87.

26. *The Great Salvation* is at hand, if you will receive it as the gift of God.
    Letter, 21/4/87.

27. Look up, and receive a fresh supply of grace.
    Letter, 2/3/73.

28. Be punctual. Do everything exactly at the time.
    Twelve Rules.

29. The Methodists must take heed to their doctrine, their experience, their practice, and their discipline.
    To Robert Miller, 1783.

30. Let your eye be single; aim still at one thing;—holy, loving faith; giving God the whole heart.
    Letter, 16/9/74.

31. And invite all to this: one love; one present and eternal heaven.
    Letter, 16/9/74.

AUGUST

1. I believe the merciful God regards the lives and tempers of men more than their ideas. I believe He respects the goodness of the heart more than the clearness of the head. *Works,* vii. 354.

2. Oh what a pearl, of how great price, is the very lowest degree of the peace of God! *Works,* xii. 170.

3. I am now nearly as I was before my illness; but, I hope, more determined to sell all for the pearl. *Letter,* 31/7/75.

4. Joy you shall have, if joy be best. *Letter,* 16/12/72.

5. The sea breezes may be of service to you, if you have constant exercise. This is beyond all medicine whatever. *Letter,* 15/9/77.

6. If those who 'gain all they can,' and 'save all they can,' will likewise 'give all they can'; then, the more they gain, the more they will grow in grace, and the more treasure they will lay up in heaven. *Works,* xiii. 261.

7. When I have an opportunity of doing good, I will permit no man to tie my hands. Reynolds' *Anecdotes of Wesley,* p. 25.

8. I can see nothing that I have done or suffered that will bear looking at. I have no other plea than this: I the chief of sinners am, but Jesus died for me.

Moore's Life, ii. 389.

9. They are no Methodists that will bear no restraints. Explain this at large to the Society.

Works, xiii. 164.

10. Can you empty the great deep drop by drop? Then you may reform us by dissuasives from particular vices.

Works, v. 15.

11. But let the 'righteousness which is of God by faith' be brought in, and so shall its proud waves be stayed.

Ibid.

12. This doctrine (entire sanctification) is the grand depositum which God has lodged with the people called Methodists; and for the sake of propagating this chiefly He appears to have raised us up.

Works, xiii. 9.

13. At all times it is of use to have a Friend to whom you can pour out your heart without any disguise or reserve.

Letter, 12/11/76.

14. Surely the people of this place [Burslem] were highly favoured. Mercy embraced them on every side.

Journal, 28/3/90.

15. When I can learn nothing else, I like to learn the names of houses and villages as I pass them. *Telford's Life, p. 272.*

16. I cannot easily part with those I love. *Letter, 22/10/77.*

17. An ounce of love is worth a pound of knowledge. *Letter, 7/11/68.*

18. Whatever you do, temporal or spiritual, do it with your might. *Letter, 25/10/76.*

19. I can impute the want of increase to nothing but want of self-denial. Without this indeed, whatever other helps they have, no believers can go forward. *Journal, 13/3/90.*

20. There is nothing more sure than that God is able and willing to give always what He gives once. *Letter, 7/5/64.*

21. Put the best construction you can on everything. You know the judge is always supposed to be on the prisoner's side. *Twelve Rules.*

22. See that both of you be as little children. Your help is laid up above in the hand of Him that loves you. *Letter, 7/5/64.*

23. Wherever a man's life confirms his doctrine, God will confirm the word of His messenger. *Letter, 21/6/84.*

24. Go on: run and never tire, till we meet in our Father's house.

Letter, 15/10/77.

25. You have a message from God to some of those, to whom no one almost dare speak the whole truth.

Letter, 11/2/75.

26. When the occasion offers break through. Speak, though it is pain and grief unto you; and it will be easier and easier.

Letter, 11/2/75.

27. You have nothing to do but to save souls. Therefore spend and be spent in this work.

Twelve Rules.

28. In religion as well as in all things else, it is use that brings perfectness.

Letter, 11/2/75.

29. Perhaps when there is least appearance, a flame will suddenly break out and you shall see the day of His Power.

Letter, 10/8/76.

30. Go always, not only to those who want you, but to those who want you most.

Twelve Rules.

31. Our main doctrines, which include all the rest, are repentance, faith, and holiness. The first of these we account the porch of religion, the next the door, the third religion itself.

SEPTEMBER

1. Go forth then, thou little child that believest in Him, and His 'right hand shall teach thee terrible things.'
Works, v. 16.

2. It is all one where we are, so we are doing the will of our Lord.
Letter, 23/4/83.

3. We are called to propagate Bible religion through the land; that is, faith working by love; holy tempers and holy lives.
Letter, 8/12/77.

4. Fear nothing; only believe. His mercy embraces you: it holds you in on every side.
Works, xii. 493.

5. Be not prejudiced against Christianity by those who know nothing at all of it.
Works, viii. 197.

6. Do a little at a time, that you may do more.
Letter, 9/2/91.

7. You will need all the grace and sense you have, and to have all your wits about you.
Twelve Rules.

8. But still God is over all!

Journal, 19/9/90.

9. I never undertake any more work than I can go through with perfect calmness of spirit.

Letter, 10/12/77.

10. Any but a particular Providence is no Providence at all.

Journal, 6/7/81.

11. Let us work now; we shall rest by-and-by.

Letter, 11/9/89.

12. I know no danger that a lover of God can be in, till God is no more, or at least has quitted the reins, and left chance to govern the world.

Letter, 12/8/31.

13. Christian Perfection is humble, gentle, patient love regulating all the tempers, and governing all the words and actions.

Letter, 11/6/77.

14. Look up, my dear friend, look up! and see your crown before you.

Letter, 15/12/90.

15. Now do all the good you can to your poor neighbours. A word spoken in season, how good is it!

Letter, 22/1/91.

16. I wonder the devil has not wisdom enough to discern that he is destroying his own kingdom.

Journal, 16/9/40.

17. Spare no pains; and God, our own God, shall give you His blessing!

Letter, 29/1/91.

18. All will follow persevering sincerity. God gives everything with it, nothing without it.

Minutes of the First Conference.

19. I am exceedingly afraid of covetousness, lest it should steal unawares, either upon myself or my friends.

Letter, 26/4/77.

20. I know no way to escape covetousness but (having saved all we can) to give all we can.

Letter, 26/4/77.

21. If you seek your happiness in God alone, you will never be disappointed; if in anything else you surely will; for all creatures are broken cisterns.

Letter, 29/1/91.

22. I love prayer-meetings, and wish they were set up in every corner of the town.

Letter, 11/12/72.

23. An immortal spirit can be satisfied with nothing but seeing God.

Journal, 2/10/90.

24. I firmly believe I am a Scriptural ἐπίσκοπος, as much as any man in England or in Europe.

Letter to C. Wesley, 19/8/85.

25. I verily think these Sunday schools are one of the noblest specimens of charity which have been set on foot since the time of William the Conqueror.

Letter, 9/1/88.

26. It is expedient that the Methodists in every part of the globe should be united together as closely as possible. That we may all be one is the prayer of your affectionate Friend and Brother.

Letter, 4/2/90.

27. There can be no little sin, till we can find a little God.

Works, vii. 116.

28. You have only to go on calmly and steadily, and God will arise and maintain His own cause.

Letter, 27/3/90.

29. The love of God is the most powerful of all means of health and long life.

Preface to 'Primitive Physic.'

30. Continually telling people they are dead is the ready way to make them so.

Journal, 13/6/71.

OCTOBER

1. *Use* the world, and *enjoy* God.
   Works, vii. 222.

2. There is the closest connexion between my religious and my political conduct.
   Letter, 25/6/77.

3. The self-same authority enjoins me to 'fear God' and to 'honour the King.'
   Letter, 25/6/77.

4. How admirably pardon and holiness are comprised in that one word, 'grace'!
   Letter, 2/4/81.

5. With what will be we have nothing to do. We need take no thought for the morrow.
   Letter, 12/2/82.

6. It seemed as if all that heard were, for the present, almost persuaded to be Christians.
   Journal, 6/10/90.

7. Had we ever a larger field of action? And shall we stand all, or any part of, the day idle?
   Letter, 2/12/67.

8. You are going the straight way to be swallowed up in God.
   Letter, 9/3/82.

9. The certain way to make each other happy
   is to strengthen each other's hands in
   God.

   Letter, 4/7/81.

10. You need not be overcome by peevishness
    any more; the grace of God is sufficient
    for you.

    Letter, 17/12/72.

11. We are always safe while we are either
    doing or suffering the will of Him that
    orders all things well.

    Letter, 30/10/82.

12. I blame all, even that speak the truth,
    otherwise than in love.

    Letter, 9/9/77.

13. Keenness of spirit and tartness of lan-
    guage are never to be commended.

    Letter, 9/9/77.

14. We are men; we are Englishmen: as
    such we have a natural and legal right to
    liberty of conscience.

    Letter, 30/11/82.

15. I pray God that you may resolutely choose
    Him for your portion.

    Letter, 31/3/81.

16. He can make you large amends for all
    He has taken away by giving you Himself.

    Letter, 23/12/82.

17. The example of those that are round about us is apt to get within our guard.

Letter, 8/9/81.

18. I doubt whether you do not undervalue some of the talents which God has lent you.

Letter, 15/11/81.

19. If you have God on your side nothing can hurt you. O consecrate your early days to Him.

Letter, 5/8/70.

20. I will thank the youngest man among you to tell me of any fault you see in me; in doing so, I shall consider him my best friend.

Methodist Magazine, 1825, p. 390.

21. I reverence the young because they may be useful after I am dead.

22. Nothing can prevent the success of this blessed work, but the neglect of the instruments.

Letter, 24/3/90.

23. We are not allowed, upon any account whatever, to render evil for evil, or railing for railing.

Letter, 9/9/77.

24. I advise you first to be a Bible Christian yourself, inwardly and outwardly.

Letter, 17/7/81.

25. I want you, not to be a half but a whole Christian.

Letter, 4/8/81.

26. It is a little thing to trust God as far as we can see Him; so far the way lies open before us.

Letter, 18/12/72.

27. But to trust Him when we are hedged in on every side, and can see no way to escape, this is good and acceptable with God.

Letter, 18/12/72.

28. We are not at liberty to impair our own health in hopes of doing good to others.

Letter, 19/11/81.

29. We must not offer murder for sacrifice.

Letter, 19/11/81.

30. There is great reason that we should trust the Invisible God farther than we can see Him.

Letter, 9/2/82.

31. You have His love, and truth, and promise on your side, and He hath never failed them that seek Him.

Letter, 28/10/77.

NOVEMBER

1. All Saints' Day, a day that I peculiarly love. *Journal, 1/11/89.*

2. Go on, in a full pursuit of all the mind that was in Christ, of inward and then outward holiness; so shall you be not almost but altogether a Christian. *Works, vii. 75.*

3. I only desire to creep on in the vale of humble love. *Letter, 26/6/88.*

4. The work of God prospers well in London. A new chapel brings almost a new congregation, and hereby the old is greatly stirred up. *Letter, 9/12/78.*

5. If you give way to discontent, it will find you in any place. *Letter, 1/6/89.*

6. My time is short: so I publish as much as I can at once, if haply I may live to finish it. *Letter, 18/10/77.*

7. Look unto Jesus! He is altogether lovely! but how little have you loved Him! *Letter, 5/7/89.*

8. I love Sunday schools much. They have done abundance of good.

Letter, 24/11/87.

9. I save all I can and give all I can; that is, all I have.

Diary, 16/7/90.

10. I entreat you not to beat me down in order to quicken my pace.

Preface to Sermons.

11. O how honourable is a beast of God's making, compared to one who makes himself a beast.

Works, xi. 169.

12. A Christian abhors sloth as much as drunkenness.

Works, v. 385.

13. I wish you to be always full of faith and love, and a pattern to all that are round about you.

Letter, 25/3/81.

14. While we live let us live in earnest.

Letter, 15/4/88.

15. Oh that I might dispute with no man!

Telford's *Life of John Wesley*, p. 328.

16. When you are met together, boldly lay hold on the promise: His word will speak and will not lie.

Letter, 21/12/87.

17. I believe just what is revealed and no more.

Letter, 17/9/88.

18. But I do not pretend to account for it, or to solve the difficulties that may attend it.

Letter, 17/9/88.

19. I do not remember to have felt lowness of spirits for a quarter of an hour since I was born.

Journal, 1780.

20. I wish to be, in every point, great and small, a scriptural, rational Christian.

Letter, 24/1/89.

21. Let all the springs of your happiness be in Him (Jesus).

Letter, 5/7/89.

22. If I had no *other* good to give, I ought at least to have given them good words.

Telford's *Life of John Wesley,* p. 332.

23. We now fear greater danger from honour than from dishonour.

Letter 14/7/89.

24. God will surely exalt us if we do not exalt ourselves.

Letter 14/7/89.

25. I am glad you use more exercise. It is good for both body and soul.

Letter, 24/1/71.

26. I sincerely desire to be better informed. I say to God and man, 'What I know not, teach Thou me.' *Preface to Sermons.*

27. When the Son of Man shall come in His glory, the brightest crown will be given to the sufferers. *Letter, 9/1/89.*

28. Look up, thou blessed one! the time is at hand. *Letter, 9/1/89.*

29. It is a blessed thing to have fellow-travellers to the New Jerusalem. *Letter, 2/8/89.*

30. Strengthen you one another. Talk to-gether as often as you can. And pray earnestly with and for one another, that you may endure to the end and be saved. *Works, viii. 249.*

DECEMBER

1. At any price give me the book of God!
I have it. Here is knowledge enough for
me. Let me be *homo unius libri* (a man
of one book).

Preface to Sermons.

2. One would hope the time is approaching
when the earth shall be filled with the
knowledge of the glory of the Lord.

Letter, 4/2/90.

3. Never imagine you and I shall be saved
from reproach unless we changed our
Master.

Letter, 28/2/90.

4. It is our part to follow the openings of
Divine Providence, and follow the leadings
of it.

Letter, March 1790.

5. I feel more want of heat than light. I
value light, but it is nothing compared
to love.

Letter, 9/6/75.

6. Let us redouble our diligence! Let us
do everything just as we would wish to
have done it, when we are stepping into
eternity.

Letter, 6/12/76.

55

7. If we do not take care we shall all degenerate into milksops.

   Letter, 13/3/90.

8. There is no happiness without Him for any child of man. One would rather choose to be pained and restless whenever He withdraws His presence.

   Letter, 1/1/70.

9. God's time is always the best time.

   Works, vi. 40.

10. Health is a great blessing.

    Letter, 6/6/90.

11. It is our duty to take care of our bodily health; but what is this to an healthful mind?

    Letter, 15/3/75.

12. Make use of the faith and talents which God hath given you, and He will give you more faith and more fruit: for there is no end to His mercies.

    Letter, 18/10/90.

13. Have pity even upon the world of the ungodly. Do not lay more stumbling-blocks in the way of those for whom Christ died. *Works,* vi. 410.

14. By confining yourself to those who write clearly, your understanding will be opened and strengthened far more than by reading a multiplicity of authors.

    Letter, 17/1/75.

15. God is willing to give always what He grants once.

Works, xii. 493.

16. Our business now is to love and obey: knowledge is reserved for eternity.

Letter, 20/7/71.

17. Put off the gentlewoman: you bear a higher character. You are an heir of God, and a joint heir with Christ.

Letter, 9/6/75.

18. You have only to go on calmly and steadily, and God will arise and maintain His cause.

Letter, 27/3/90.

19. There is nothing deeper, there is nothing better, in heaven or earth, than love.

Letter, 17/1/75.

20. As to all opinions which do not strike at the root of Christianity, we think and let think.

Works, viii. 340.

21. Let us use the short residue of life to the glory of Him who gave it.

Letter, 28/7/75.

22. Love the creature as it leads to the Creator.

Sermon XIII, §I, 12.

23. By the grace of God I shall go on, following peace with all men.

Letter, 18/2/75.

24. Christianity is essentially a social religion: and to turn it into a solitary one is to destroy it.

Works, v. 297.

25. In the fullness of time He was made Man, another common head of mankind, a second general parent, and representative of the whole human race.

Works, v. 55.

26. We have only to live to-day! God will take care of to-morrow.

Letter, 28/7/75.

27. Life is a few days in a strange land; then think and let think.

Letter to Bishop of Lincoln.

28. Surely the man that may die to-night should live to-day.

Wesley Studies, p. 202.

29. Be zealous! Be active! Time is short.

Letter, 17/2/91.

30. I want to know one thing—the way to heaven; how to land safe on that happy shore.

Preface to Sermons.

31. I have thought, I am a creature of a day, passing through life as an arrow through the air. I am a spirit come from God, and returning to God.

Preface to Sermons.

PORTRAITS AND SELECTIONS

In those clear, piercing, piteous eyes behold
The very soul that over England flamed!
Deep, pure, intense; consuming shame and ill:
Convicting men of sin; making faith live;
And—this the mightiest miracle of all—
Creating God again in human hearts.
                              —R. W. GILDER.

THE BLOOD OF THE POOR

MANY years ago, when I was at Oxford, in a cold winter's day, a young maid (one of those we kept at school) called upon me. I said, ' You seem half-starved. Have you nothing to cover you but that thin linen gown?' She said, ' Sir, this is all I have!' I put my hand in my pocket, but found I had scarce any money left, having just paid away what I had. It immediately struck me, ' Will thy Master say, "Well done, good and faithful steward? Thou hast adorned thy walls with the money which might have screened this poor creature from the cold!" O justice! O mercy! Are not these pictures the blood of this poor maid?' See thy expensive apparel in the same light; thy gown, hat, head-dress! Everything about thee which cost more than Christian duty required thee to lay out is the blood of the poor! O be wise for the time to come! Be more merciful! more faithful to God and man! more abundantly *adorned* (like men and women professing godliness) *with good works!*

Sermon on Dress, *Works,* vii, 21.

I.

The First-known Portrait

THIS engraving on copper, which is very rare, only one other copy being known, was lent for reproduction by Mr. George Stampe from his unique collection of Wesley Portraits. He says : 'It is a very fine bit of engraving, and is, I believe, the first engraved portrait, and was issued in 1741. It is quite in George Vertue's style, and was probably done by him, though the features in no way resemble those in the three separate folio engravings of Wesley made by Vertue in 1745, all of which I have. . . . This copy was given to me by my late dear friend, the Rev. Richard Green, about a year before he died.'

The First-known Portrait.

BEGINS HIS EARLY RISING

If any one desires to know exactly what quantity of sleep his own constitution requires, he may very easily make the experiment which I made about sixty years ago. I then waked every night about twelve or one, and lay awake for some time. I readily concluded that this arose from my lying longer in bed than nature required. To be satisfied, I procured an alarum, which waked me the next morning at seven (near an hour earlier than I rose the day before); yet I lay awake again at night. The second morning I rose at six; but, notwithstanding this, I lay awake the second night. The third morning I rose at five; but, nevertheless, I lay awake the third night. The fourth morning I rose at four (as, by the grace of God, I have done ever since); and I lay awake no more. And I do not now lie awake (taking the year round) a quarter of an hour together in a month. By the same experiment, rising earlier and earlier every morning, may any one find how much sleep he really wants.

Sermon, On Redeeming the Time, *Works*, vii. 69.

5

II.

The Portrait by Williams

THE portrait by John Michael
Williams, R.A., is generally regarded
as the best likeness of Wesley in
early life. This well-known picture,
the original of which is at Didsbury
College, was painted in 1742. It represents Wesley in gown and bands,
standing with both hands resting on
a book. It has been many times engraved and otherwise reproduced.
Williams afterwards painted another
portrait, in which the bust only is
shown; and a copy of this, in oils,
hangs in the Book Steward's room at
the Wesleyan Conference Office. It
is from this painting that our reproduction is made.

The Portrait by Williams.

GAINING, SAVING, GIVING

PERMIT me to speak as freely of myself as I would of another man. I *gain all I can* (namely, by writing) without hurting either my soul or body. I *save all I can*, not willingly wasting anything, not a sheet of paper, not a cup of water. I do not lay out anything, not a shilling, unless as a sacrifice to God. Yet by *giving all I can*, I am effectually secured from ' laying up treasures upon earth.' Yea, and I am secured from either desiring or endeavouring it, as long as I give all I can. And that I do this, I call all that know me, both friends and foes, to testify.

Sermon, On The Danger of Riches, *Works*, vii. 9.

III.

The Portrait by Vertue

GEORGE VERTUE (1684-1756) was a famous engraver of historical portraits. Horace Walpole, in his *Anecdotes of Painting,* says he executed two prints of John Wesley. The first was drawn from life and engraved by Vertue in 1742; in 1745 he issued a second portrait with somewhat altered features. This is shown opposite. There is a third engraving by Vertue in which the face is reproduced from the Williams portrait. Vertue was buried in the cloisters of Westminster Abbey.

The Portrait by Vertue.

A FORM OF PRAYER

O THOU who art 'the Way, the Truth, and the Life,' Thou hast said no man can follow Thee, unless he renounce himself. I know, O Saviour, that Thou hast laid nothing upon us but what the design of Thy love made necessary for us. Thou sawest our disease, our idolatrous self-love, whereby we fell away from God, to be as gods ourselves, to please ourselves, and to do our own will. Lo, I come! May I ever renounce my own, and do Thy blessed will in all things!

O Thou, whose whole life did cry aloud, 'Father, not Mine, but Thy will be done,' give me grace to walk after Thy pattern, to tread in Thy steps. Give me grace to 'take up my cross daily,' to inure myself to bear hardship. Let me now practise what is not pleasing to flesh and blood, what is not agreeable to my senses, appetites, and passions, that I may not hereafter renounce Thee, for fear of suffering for Thee, but may stand firm in the 'day of my visitation.'

Works, xi. 219.

IV.

Another Early Portrait

THIS portrait of Wesley, apparently
in early middle life, is supposed to
have been issued by the Moravians.
The original engraving is enclosed in
an oval design, set on a pedestal
adorned with books, and bears a
scroll containing the following verse :

His eyes diffuse a venerable grace,
And Charity itself is in his face;
Humble and meek, learned, pious, pru-
    dent, just,
Of good report, and faithful to his trust;
Vigilant, sober, watchful of his charge,
Who feeds his sheep, and doth their folds
    enlarge.

These lines are stated to have been
written by his eldest sister, Emilia.
The portrait was 'sold against Birchin
Lane, in Cornhill, price 6d.' Its size
was 12¼ by 9¼ ins.

Another Early Portrait.

THE DAY AFTER HIS CONVERSION

THE moment I awaked, ' Jesus, Master,' was in my heart and in my mouth; and I found all my strength lay in keeping my eye fixed upon Him, and my soul waiting on Him continually. Being again at St. Paul's in the afternoon, I could taste the good word of God in the anthem, which began, ' My song shall be always of the loving kindness of the Lord: with my mouth will I ever be showing forth Thy truth from one generation to another.' Yet the enemy injected a fear, ' If thou dost believe, why is there not a more sensible change? ' I answered (yet not I), ' That I know not. But this I know, I have " now peace with God." And I sin not to-day, and Jesus my Master has forbid me to take thought for the morrow.'

' But is not any sort of fear,' continued the tempter, ' a proof that thou dost not believe? ' I desired my Master to answer for me; and opened His Book upon those words of St. Paul, ' Without were fightings, within were fears.' Then, inferred I, well may fears be within me; but I must go on, and tread them under my feet.

Journal, May 25, 1738.

V.

John Downes' First Portrait

JOHN DOWNES was a Methodist preacher from 1743 to 1774. Wesley considered him 'by nature full as great a genius as Sir Isaac Newton.' He made himself tools and proceeded to make the engraving of the Williams' portrait here reproduced. Copies of this are now extremely rare. Downes afterwards executed a larger engraving of the same portrait, which forms the frontispiece to the first edition of Wesley's *Notes on the New Testament* (see p. 157). He died suddenly after preaching at West Street Chapel, on November 4, 1774.

John Downes' First Portrait.

BOOKS FOR THE PEOPLE

Two-and-Forty years ago, having a desire to furnish poor people with cheaper, shorter, and plainer books than any I had seen, I wrote many small tracts, generally a penny a-piece; and afterwards several larger. Some of these had such a sale as I never thought of; and, by this means, I unawares became rich. But I never desired or endeavoured after it. And now that it is come upon me unawares, I lay up no treasures upon earth: I lay up nothing at all. My desire and endeavour, in this respect, is to 'wind my bottom round the year.'* I cannot help leaving my books behind me whenever God calls me hence; but, in every other respect, my own hands will be my executors.

Sermon, On The Danger of Riches, *Works*, vii. 9.

*Each Christmas they accompts did clear,
And wound their bottom round the year.
                    Prior: *An Epitaph.*

VI.

The Portrait by Tinney

JOHN TINNEY, who engraved the fine
mezzotint from which this portrait
is taken, was an English engraver,
who set up a business in Fleet Street
in the mid-eighteenth century. This
was one of his latest portraits, and it
was probably published between 1750
and 1760. It will be noticed that
there is a sort of family likeness to
the Williams type of portrait. Copies
of the engraving are exceedingly
scarce, 'only four being known to
collectors,' says Mr. J. G. Wright.

The Portrait by Tinney.

ELECTRICITY AS A MEDICINE

HAVING procured an apparatus on purpose, I ordered several persons to be electrified, who were ill of various disorders; some of whom found an immediate, some a gradual, cure. From this time I appointed, first some hours in every week, and afterward an hour in every day, wherein any that desired it might try the virtue of this surprising medicine. Two or three years after, our patients were so numerous that we were obliged to divide them. So part were electrified in Southwark, part at the Foundery, others near St. Paul's, and the rest near the Seven-Dials. The same method we have taken ever since; and to this day, while hundreds, perhaps thousands, have received unspeakable good, I have not known one man, woman, or child, who has received any hurt thereby. So that when I hear any talk of the danger of being electrified (especially if they are medical men who talk so), I cannot but impute it to great want either of sense or honesty.

Journal, November 9, 1756.

VII.

The Zoffany Portrait

THIS was executed in oils by Johann Zoffany, probably about the year 1760. The artist came to England, where he lived in obscurity and poverty for some time, but rose to such eminence that George III and his consort sat to him, and five of his paintings are in the National Portrait Gallery. A copy of the portrait was made many years later by Sylvester Harding and engraved by W. N. Gardiner, an Irish worker of some repute. Zoffany went to India, amassed a fortune, returned to England, and died at Kew in 1810. The original painting belongs to the Rev. M. Riggall, who has kindly allowed a photograph of it to be reproduced.

The Zoffany Portrait.

VIEWS ON HISTORY

I FINISHED *Historic Doubts on the Life and Reign of Richard the Third*. What an amazing monster, both in body and mind, have our historians and poets painted him! And yet I think Mr. Walpole makes it more clear than one could expect at this distance of time: 1. That he was not only not remarkably deformed, but, on the contrary, remarkably handsome. 2. That his Queen, whom he entirely loved, died a natural death. 3. That his nephew, Edward the Fifth, did so too; there being no shadow of proof to the contrary. 4. That his other nephew, Richard, was the very person whom Henry the Seventh murdered, after constraining him to call himself Perkin Warbeck. 5. That the death of his brother, the Duke of Clarence, was the sole act, not of him, but Edward the Fourth. 6. That he had no hand at all in the murder of Henry the Sixth, any more than of his son. And, lastly, that he was clear of all blame as to the execution of Lord Hastings; as well as of Rivers, Grey, and Vaughan. What a surprising thing is it, then, that all our historians should have so readily swallowed the account of that wretch who 'killed, and also took possession' of the throne; and blundered on, one after another! Only it is to be observed, for fifty years no one could contradict that account, but at the peril of his head.

Journal, June 17, 1769.

VIII.

The Portrait by Hunter

THIS portrait, by Robert Hunter, was engraved by James Watson, and is one of the finest examples of the engraver's art in dark mezzotint. As a portrait of Wesley, however, it can only be called a caricature. The artist was a well-known portrait painter in Dublin during the latter half of the eighteenth century, and was a friend of Wesley, who spoke of the work with a wealth of praise that few of us can endorse. Watson was a member of a family famous as engravers in mezzotint, and who reproduced many of the best works of Sir Joshua Reynolds. The engraving is now scarce, and the original painting has been lost sight of.

The Portrait by Hunter.

WORSHIP OF SELF

INDEED it may be said that every man
is by nature, as it were, his own god.
He worships himself. He is, in his own
conception, absolute lord of himself.
Dryden's hero speaks only according to
nature, when he says, 'Myself am king of
me.' He seeks himself in all things. He
pleases himself. And why not? Who
is lord over him? *His own will* is his
only law; he does this or that because it
is his good pleasure. In the same spirit
as the 'son of the morning' said in old
time, 'I will sit upon the sides of the
North,' he says, '*I will* do thus or thus.'
And do we not find sensible men on every
side who are of the self-same spirit? who,
if asked, 'Why did you do this?' will
readily answer, 'Because I had a mind
to it.'

Sermon, On the Education of Children, *Works,* vii. 89.

IX.

The Portrait by Hone

THE original of this picture hangs in the National Portrait Gallery. It was painted in 1765 by Nathaniel Hone, R.A., who is known principally as a miniaturist. The portrait has been several times engraved. Our reproduction is from the engraving by Bland which formed the frontispiece to Wesley's *Notes on the Old Testament*. The portrait was also issued reversed, the face looking the opposite way and the *left* hand held up. This has led to the conjecture that Hone may have painted two portraits.

The Portrait by Hone.

PLAIN TRUTH FOR PLAIN PEOPLE

I DESIGN plain truth for plain people. Therefore, of set purpose, I abstain from all nice and philosophical speculations; from all perplexed and intricate reasonings; and, as far as possible, from even the show of learning, unless in sometimes citing the original Scripture. I labour to avoid all words which are not easy to be understood, all which are not used in common life; and, in particular, those kinds of technical terms that so frequently occur in Bodies of Divinity; those modes of speaking which men of reading are intimately acquainted with, but which to common people are an unknown tongue. Yet I am not assured that I do not sometimes slide into them unawares. It is so extremely natural to imagine that a word which is familiar to ourselves is so to all the world.

Preface to Sermons, *Works*, v. 2.

X.

The Portrait by Russell

THE original of this picture is stated to be in the dining-hall at Kingswood School (but see p. 242). It was painted in 1773 by John Russell, R.A. (1745-1806). The artist is said to have been converted under Charles Wesley's preaching, and for some years attended City Road and West Street Chapels. He was the first Methodist R.A., John Jackson being the second. The reproduction given is from a mezzotint by Bland. Charles Wesley's elder son and his daughter were staying with the Russells at Guildford in October, 1777. See C. Wesley's *Journal,* &c., ii. 276.

191043

The Portrait by Russell.

A MAN OF ONE BOOK

To candid, reasonable men, I am not afraid to lay open what have been the inmost thoughts of my heart. I have thought, I am a creature of a day, passing through life as an arrow through the air. I am a spirit come from God, and returning to God: just hovering over the great gulf; till, a few moments hence, I am no more seen; I drop into an unchangeable eternity! I want to know one thing,—the way to heaven; how to land safe on that happy shore. God Himself has condescended to teach the way: for this very end He came from heaven. He hath written it down in a book. O give me that book! At any price, give me the book of God! I have it. Here is knowledge enough for me. Let me be *homo unius libri*.* Here, then, I am, far from the busy ways of men. I sit down alone: only God is here. In His presence I open, I read His book; for this end, to find the way to heaven.

Preface to Sermons, *Works,* v. 2.

* A man of one book.

XI.

The 'J. Johnson' Portrait

THIS engraving was drawn and published by T. Holloway in 1776. It was used in 1791 as the frontispiece to Hampson's *Life* of Wesley, where it is stated to be published by J. Johnson, St. Paul's Churchyard, on April 25, 1791, 'as the Act directs.' Our reproduction is slightly larger than the original.

The 'J. Johnson' Portrait.

EXPERIMENTAL RELIGION

I HAVE accordingly set down in the following sermons what I find in the Bible concerning the way to heaven; with a view to distinguish this way of God from all those which are the inventions of men. I have endeavoured to describe the true, the scriptural, experimental religion, so as to omit nothing which is a real part thereof, and to add nothing thereto which is not. And herein it is more especially my desire, first, to guard those who are just setting their faces toward heaven (and who, having little acquaintance with the things of God, are the more liable to be turned out of the way), from formality, from mere outside religion, which has almost driven heart-religion out of the world; and, secondly, to warn those who know the religion of the heart, the faith which worketh by love, lest at any time they make void the law through faith, and so fall back into the snare of the devil.

Preface to Sermons, *Works,* v. 4.

XII.

The 'Arminian Magazine' Portrait

THIS portrait was issued with the
first volume of the *Arminian Magazine*. It is not regarded as a good
likeness of Wesley, though, as he
admitted it into his own magazine,
we are bound to assume that he must
have been fairly satisfied with it.
Some copies of the volume contained
another and more prepossessing sub-
stitute, but this latter plate is exceedingly rare. Another and smaller
portrait of Wesley appeared in the
Magazine for 1783 (see page 115).

The 'Arminian Magazine' Portrait.

ENGLAND'S UNGODLINESS

SEE, then, Englishmen, what is the undoubted characteristic of our nation; it is ungodliness. True, it was not always so. For many ages we had as much of the fear of God as our neighbours. But in the last age, many who were absolute strangers to this made so large a profession of it, that the nation in general was surfeited, and, at the Restoration, ran headlong from one extreme to the other. It was then ungodliness broke in upon us as a flood; and when shall its dire waves be stayed?

Countrymen, is ungodliness any honour to our nation? Let men of reason judge. Is this outraging the Greatest and Best of beings, a thing honourable in itself? Surely you cannot think so. Does it gain us any honour in the eyes of other nations? Nay, just the contrary. Some of them abhor the very name of Englishmen, others despise us, on this very account. They look upon us as monsters, hardly worthy to be ranked among human creatures,

Works, xi. p. 162.

XIII.

The 'Gainer' Portrait

THIS portrait is from a mezzotint
engraving by John Gainer, and was
published on April 20, 1779, when
Wesley was in his seventy-sixth year.
Mr. J. G. Wright (*Proceedings*, Wesley
ley Historical Society, iv., 1-5) had
seen only two copies of this engraving, one in the Salt Library at Stafford, the other in the Allan Library.
Size 12 inches by 9.

The 'Gainer' Portrait.

A DESCRIPTION OF THE METHODISTS

By Methodists I mean a people who profess to pursue (in whatsoever measure they have attained) holiness of heart and life, inward and outward conformity in all things to the revealed will of God; who place religion in an uniform resemblance of the great object of it; in a steady imitation of Him they worship, in all His imitable perfections; more particularly, in justice, mercy, and truth, or universal love filling the heart, and governing the life.

You, to whom I now speak, believe this love of human kind cannot spring but from the love of God. You think there can be no instance of one whose tender affection embraces every child of man (though not endeared to him either by ties of blood, or by any natural or civil relation), unless that affection flow from a grateful, filial love to the common Father of all; to God, considered not only as his Father, but as 'the Father of the spirits of all flesh'; yea, as the general Parent and Friend of all the families both of heaven and earth.

Works, viii. 352.

XIV.

Another 'Magazine' Portrait

WESLEY himself inserted this portrait in the *Arminian Magazine* for 1783 (Vol. VI). Mr. J. G. Wright thought that neither the engraver's skill nor Wesley's judgement in allowing it to appear was beyond criticism—an opinion which many others will uphold.

Another 'Magazine' Portrait.

ADVICE TO METHODISTS

You believe, farther, that both this faith and love are wrought in us by the Spirit of God; nay, that there cannot be in any man one good temper or desire, or so much as one good thought, unless it be produced by the almighty power of God, by the inspiration or influence of the Holy Ghost.

If you walk by this rule, continually endeavouring to know and love and resemble and obey the great God and Father of our Lord Jesus Christ, as the God of Love, or pardoning mercy; if from this principle of loving, obedient faith, you carefully abstain from all evil, and labour, as you have opportunity, to do good to all men, friends or enemies; if, lastly, you unite together, to encourage and help each other in thus working out your salvation, and for that end watch over one another in love, you are they whom I mean by Methodists.

Works, viii. 352.

XV.

The Dornford-Cummins
Portrait

WESLEY, while on a visit to Deptford in his eighty-second year, was prevailed upon by his friend Josiah Dornford to have his portrait taken. By his will Mr. Dornford left this painting to his executor, Mr. Jonah Freeman. It was afterwards taken to Australia, and for many years was in the possession of Mrs. Cummins, of New South Wales, who in 1906 presented it to the British Wesleyan Conference. It is now at the Book Room. The name of the artist is unknown; but it greatly resembles the portrait by Horsley, now hanging at Richmond College (see page 143).

The Dornford-Cummins Portrait.

WILLINGNESS TO BE LED

ARE you persuaded you see more clearly than me? It is not unlikely that you may. Then treat me as you would desire to be treated yourself upon a change of circumstances. Point me out a better way than I have yet known. Show me it is so, by plain proof of Scripture. And if I linger in the path I have been accustomed to tread, and am therefore unwilling to leave it, labour with me a little; take me by the hand, and lead me as I am able to bear. But be not displeased if I entreat you not to beat me down in order to quicken my pace: I can go but feebly and slowly at best; then, I should not be able to go at all. May I not request of you, further, not to give me hard names in order to bring me into the right way. Suppose I were ever so much in the wrong, I doubt this would not set me right. Rather, it would make me run so much the farther from you, and so get more and more out of the way.

Preface to Sermons, *Works*, v. 5.

XVI.

The Portrait by Hamilton

WILLIAM HAMILTON, R.A. (1751-1801), was an artist of versatile attainments, although not accounted an excellent portrait-painter. The original painting is in the National Portrait Gallery. It represents Wesley at eighty-five, and the entry in the *Journal* for December 22, 1787, is supposed to refer to it: 'I yielded to the importunity of a painter, and sat an hour and a half in all for my picture. I think it was the best that ever was taken.' The reproduction here is from the engraving by James Fittler, which was published in 1788.

The Portrait by Hamilton.

AVOID AN ANGRY SPIRIT

NAY, perhaps, if you are angry, so shall I be too; and then there will be small hopes of finding the truth. If once anger arise, ἠΰτε καπνος,* (as Homer somewhere expresses it), this smoke will so dim the eyes of my soul, that I shall be able to see nothing clearly. For God's sake, if it be possible to avoid it, let us not provoke one another to wrath. Let us not kindle in each other this fire of hell; much less blow it up into a flame. If we could discern truth by that dreadful light, would it not be loss, rather than gain? For, how far is love, even with many wrong opinions, to be preferred before truth itself without love! We may die without the knowledge of many truths, and yet be carried into Abraham's bosom. But, if we die without love, what will knowledge avail? Just as much as it avails the devil and his angels!

Preface to Sermons, *Works,* v. 5.

* Like smoke.

XVII.

The Portrait by Romney

THIS portrait is generally regarded
as the best taken in Wesley's later
years. Wesley sat to Romney on
January 5, 1789 (see *Journal* under
date). It was engraved by two well-
known artists, Spilsbury and Ward.
The reproduction opposite is from
Spilsbury's engraving. Romney
painted two replicas of the portrait.
The original is now in Philadelphia.
George Romney (1734-1802) was a
celebrated painter, earning as much
as £4,000 during one year from his
portraits alone; and according to
Flaxman, was 'the first of all our
painters for poetic dignity of
conception.' A reproduction of the
Romney portrait by George Baxter
appears as frontispiece to this
volume. Baxter had close connexion with Methodism between 1840
and 1850.

The Portrait by Romney.

FREE GRACE

ALL the blessings which God hath bestowed upon man are of His mere grace, bounty, or favour; His free, undeserved favour; favour altogether undeserved; man having no claim to the least of His mercies. It was free grace that 'formed man of the dust of the ground, and breathed into him a living soul,' and stamped on that soul the image of God, and 'put all things under his feet.' The same free grace continues to us, at this day, life, and breath, and all things. For there is nothing we are, or have, or do, which can deserve the least thing at God's hand. 'All our works, Thou, O God, hast wrought in us.' These, therefore, are so many more instances of free mercy. And whatever righteousness may be found in man, this is also the gift of God.

Sermon on Salvation by Faith, *Works*, v. 7.

XVIII.

The 'Benjamin West' Portrait

THIS painting is signed by Benjamin West (1738-1820) in the upper left-hand corner, ' B. W.,1789.' It now belongs to Mr. Guy M. Walker of New York, who found beneath the edge of the frame a card with the words, ' Rev. John Wesley, painted at Doncaster, a little time before his death. Bought by Mr. A. Moir, Mildmay Park, March, 1863.' Mr. Walker bought it from Mr. Smith, whose mother's brother, Mr. Simpson, was a noted evangelist, and acquired the portrait when on a visit to England.

The 'Benjamin West' Portrait.

A SENSE OF SIN

'THAT you may have a full view of the sin of your nature, I would recommend to you three things: 1. Study to know the spirituality and the extent of the law of God; for that is the glass wherein you may see yourselves. 2. Observe your hearts at all times; but especially under temptation. Temptation is a fire that brings up the scum of the unregenerate heart. 3. Go to God through Jesus Christ, for illumination by His Spirit. Say unto Him, 'What I know not, teach Thou me!' and be willing to take in light from the word. It is by the word the Spirit teacheth; but unless He teach, all other teaching is to little purpose. You will never see yourself aright, till He light His candle in your breast. Neither the fullness and glory of Christ, nor the corruption and vileness of our nature, ever were, or can be, rightly learned, but where the Spirit of Christ is the teacher.

Works, ix. 464.

XIX.

A Portrait in Wax

THIS portrait was embossed and modelled in wax by E. Percy, 1788, and is contained in an oval frame 9½ by 8 ins. in size. It was purchased a few years ago at the sale of the Baroness Burdett-Coutts' collection, and is a beautiful example of the modeller's art.

A Portrait in Wax.

SAVING FAITH

WHAT faith is it, then, through which we are saved? It may be answered, first, in general, it is a faith in Christ: Christ, and God through Christ, are the proper objects of it. Herein, therefore, it is sufficiently, absolutely distinguished from the faith either of ancient or modern heathens. And from the faith of a devil it is fully distinguished by this,—it is not barely a speculative, rational thing, a cold, lifeless assent, a train of ideas in the head; but also a disposition of the heart. For thus saith the Scripture, 'With the heart man believeth unto righteousness'; and, 'If thou shalt confess with thy mouth the Lord Jesus, and shalt believe with thy heart, that God hath raised Him from the dead, thou shalt be saved.'

Sermon on Salvation by Faith, *Works,* v. 9.

XX.

The Portrait by Arnold

THIS portrait, executed as a miniature on ivory, is stated by Mr. G. J.
Stevenson to be that to which Wesley
refers in his *Journal* for Feb. 24,
1790 : 'I submitted to importunity,
and once more sat for my picture. I
could scarcely believe myself. The
picture of one in his eighty-seventh
year!' The portrait was engraved by
William Ridley, and used as the
frontispiece to Benson's edition of
Wesley's *Works* (1809-13). It has
more than once been wrongly attributed to Henry Edridge. The
original miniature was some years
ago in the possession of Mr. J. Lam-
bert Jones, of Dublin.

The Portrait by Arnold.

THE NEW BIRTH

THIS, then, is the salvation which is through faith, even in the present world: A salvation from sin, and the consequences of sin, both often expressed in the word *justification;* which, taken in the largest sense, implies a deliverance from guilt and punishment, by the atonement of Christ actually applied to the soul of the sinner now believing on Him, and a deliverance from the power of sin, through Christ *formed in his heart.* So that he who is thus justified, or saved by faith, is indeed *born again.* He is *born again of the Spirit* unto a new life, which 'is hid with Christ in God.' And as a new-born babe, he gladly receives the ἄδολον, '*sincere* milk of the word, and grows thereby'; going on in the might of the Lord his God, from faith to faith, from grace to grace, until, at length, he come unto 'a perfect man, unto the measure of the stature of the fullness of Christ.'

Sermon on Salvation by Faith, *Works,* v. II.

XXI.

The 'Horsley' Portrait

PAINTED from life in 1790 by
Thomas Horsley of Sunderland, a
pupil of Romney. It is now at
Richmond College, having been presented to the College by a former
student in 1863. A replica, somewhat
varied in detail, is preserved at Sans
Street Chapel, Sunderland.

The 'Horsley' Portrait.

THE INWARD WITNESS

MEANTIME, let it be observed, I do
not mean hereby, that the Spirit of God
testifies this by any outward voice; no,
nor always by an inward voice, although
He may do this sometimes. Neither do I
suppose that He always applies to the
heart (though He often may) one or more
texts of Scripture. But He so works upon
the soul by His immediate influence, and
by a strong, though inexplicable operation,
that the stormy wind and troubled waves
subside, and there is a sweet calm; the
heart resting as in the arms of Jesus, and
the sinner being clearly satisfied that God
is reconciled, that all his 'iniquities are
forgiven, and his sins covered.'

Sermon on The Witness of the Spirit,
Works, v. 125.

XXII.

The 'Miller-Hancock' Portrait

DRAWN by L. Miller, engraved by R. Hancock in December 1790, and published by H. Humphrey, Old Bond Street. At the top of the oval border are the words, 'He went about doing good.'

The 'Miller-Hancock' Portrait.

THE ALMOST CHRISTIAN

AWAKE, then, thou that sleepest, and call upon thy God. Call in the day when He may be found. Let Him not rest, till He make 'His goodness to pass before thee,' till He proclaim unto thee the name of the Lord: 'The Lord, the Lord God, merciful and gracious, long-suffering, and abundant in goodness and truth, keeping mercy for thousands, forgiving iniquity, and transgression, and sin.' Let no man persuade thee, by vain words, to rest short of this prize of thy high calling. But cry unto Him day and night, who, 'while we were without strength, died for the ungodly,' until thou knowest in whom thou hast believed, and canst say, 'My Lord, and my God!' Remember, 'always to pray, and not to faint,' till thou also canst lift up thy hand unto heaven, and declare to Him that liveth for ever and ever, 'Lord, Thou knowest all things, Thou knowest that I love Thee.'

Sermon on The Almost Christian, *Works,* v. 24.

XXIII.

The Portrait by Edridge

THIS portrait is supposed to represent Wesley in his eighty-eighth year, and is thought by some to be the last that was taken before his death. It was engraved by William Ridley, and formed the frontispiece to Coke and Moore's *Life*. It was reproduced as the frontispiece to the eighth volume of the Standard Edition of the *Journal*. Henry Edridge, R.A., the artist, was born in 1769, and admitted as a student of the Royal Academy in 1784. He practised chiefly as a miniature painter. He was made an Associate of the R.A. in 1820, and died in 1821.

The Portrait by Edridge.

A LIVING SACRIFICE

OTHER sacrifices from us He would not; but the living sacrifice of the heart He hath chosen. Let it be continually offered up to God through Christ, in flames of holy love. And let no creature be suffered to share with Him. For He is a jealous God. His throne will He not divide with another: He will reign without a rival. Be no design, no desire admitted there, but what has Him for its ultimate object. . . . For then, and not till then, is that 'mind in us which was also in Christ Jesus'; when, in every motion of our heart, in every word of our tongue, in every work of our hands, we 'pursue nothing but in relation to Him, and in subordination to His pleasure'; when we, too, neither think, nor speak, nor act, to fulfil our 'own will, but the will of Him that sent us'; when, whether we 'eat or drink, or whatever we do, we do all to the glory of God.'

Sermon on The Circumcision of the Heart, *Works*, v. 211.

XXIV.

The Portrait by Barry

THIS portrait was painted as a miniature. John Barry (who first exhibited at the Royal Academy in 1794), is said to have painted it from the life and to have made two copies. The engraving from which the above reproduction is taken was executed by James Fittler, and it formed the frontispiece to Whitehead's *Life of Wesley*. Barry's portrait is notable as being the one first issued with *Wesley's Hymns,* in the edition of 1825. There is much similarity between this picture and Arnold's (p. 139), and it was probably painted about the same time.

The Portrait by Barry.

GENIUS OF JOHN DOWNES

I SUPPOSE he was by nature full as great a genius as Sir Isaac Newton. I will mention but two or three instances of it. When he was at school, learning algebra, he came one day to his master, and said, ' Sir, I can prove this proposition a better way than it is proved in the book.' His master thought it could not be, but, upon trial, acknowledged it to be so. Some time after, his father sent him to Newcastle with a clock, which was to be mended. He observed the clockmaker's tools, and the manner how he took it in pieces and put it together again, and, when he came home, first made himself tools, and then made a clock, which went as true as any in the town. I suppose such strength of genius as this has scarce been known in Europe before.

Another proof of it was this : Thirty years ago, while I was shaving, he was whittling the top of a stick. I asked, ' What are you doing? ' He answered, ' I am taking your face, which I intend to engrave on a copper plate.' Accordingly, without any instruction, he first made himself tools, and then engraved the plate. The second picture which he engraved was that which was prefixed to the *Notes upon the New Testament*. Such another instance, I suppose, not all England, or perhaps Europe, can produce. (See p. 78.)

Journal, Nov. 4, 1774.

XXV.

The 'European Magazine' Portrait

An account of Wesley appeared in the *European Magazine* for July, August, and September, 1789, and in March, 1791. Immediately after his death the portrait given above was inserted. This was engraved by Bromley, perhaps from a painting now in the possession of Rev. Marmaduke Riggall. The name of the painter is unknown. William Bromley, the engraver, was born in 1769, and died in 1842. He was employed for many years by the trustees of the British Museum in engraving the Elgin Marbles, after drawings by Corbould.

The 'European Magazine' Portrait.

TRIBUTE TO WHITEFIELD

I MAY close this head with observing what an honour it pleased God to put upon His faithful servant, by allowing him to declare His everlasting gospel in so many various countries, to such numbers of people, and with so great an effect on so many of their precious souls! Have we read or heard of any person since the Apostles, who testified the gospel of the grace of God through so widely extended a space, through so large a part of the habitable world? Have we read or heard of any person who called so many thousands, so many myriads, of sinners to repentance? Above all, have we read or heard of any who has been a blessed instrument in His hand of bringing so many sinners from 'darkness to light, and from the power of Satan unto God?' It is true, were we to talk thus to the gay world, we should be judged to speak as barbarians. But *you* understand the language of the country to which you are going, and whither our dear friend is gone a little before us.

Sermon on the death of the Rev. George Whitefield, *Works*, vi. 177.

XXVI.

The 'Tookey' Portrait

THIS line engraving was brought
out by J. Tookey a month after
Wesley's death in 1791. Many other
portraits—good, bad, and indifferent—
issued from the press at this period.

The 'Tookey' Portrait.

THE SAINTLY FLETCHER

FOR many years I despaired of finding any inhabitant of Great Britain that could stand in any degree of comparison with Gregory Lopez, or Monsieur de Renty. But let any impartial person judge if Mr. Fletcher was at all inferior to them. Did he not experience as deep communion with God, and as high a measure of inward holiness, as was experienced by either one or the other of those burning and shining lights? And it is certain, his outward light shone before men with full as bright a lustre as theirs. But if any would draw a parallel between them, there are two circumstances which should be well observed. One is, we are not assured that the writers of their lives did not extenuate, if not suppress, their faults. . . . But I have not suppressed, or even extenuated, anything in Mr. Fletcher's life. Indeed, I know nothing that needed to be extenuated, much less to be suppressed. A second circumstance is, that the writers of their lives could not have so full a knowledge of them as I, and much more Mrs. Fletcher, had; being eye and ear witnesses of his whole conduct. Consequently, we knew that his life was not sullied with any taint of idolatry or superstition.

Works, xi. p. 364.

XXVII.

The Portrait by Holloway

THOMAS HOLLOWAY (1748-1827), whose father's name was on the first class-book at the Foundery, drew and engraved this portrait immediately after Wesley's death in 1791. It was also issued in the *Literary Magazine* in 1792, and the reproduction opposite is taken from that engraving. Holloway was a skilful line engraver, and executed many portraits of distinguished Dissenting preachers. He is said to have been employed by Wesley to engrave some of the early portraits in the *Arminian Magazine*. His chief work was an elaborate set of the cartoons of Raphael.

The Portrait by Holloway.

WESLEY'S TRIBUTE TO FLETCHER

I WAS intimately acquainted with him for thirty years. I conversed with him morning, noon, and night, without the least reserve, during a journey of many hundred miles; and in all that time I never heard him speak an improper word or saw him do an improper action. To conclude: Within fourscore years, I have known many excellent men, holy in heart and life. But one equal to him, I have not known; one so uniformly and deeply devoted to God. So unblamable a man, in every respect, I have not found either in Europe or America. Nor do I expect to find another such on this side eternity.

Works, xi. 365.

XXVIII.

The Portrait by Vaslet

An engraving by John Jones, from a drawing by Lewis Vaslet, a miniature painter of York and Bath, was published three months after Wesley's death. In Wesley's later *Diary* (1782-90) there are entries which show that when at Bath he visited the home of the Vaslets. Both the original drawing (now at the Mission House) and the engraving executed from it were most unflattering reproductions of Wesley; and the portrait given here is from a re-drawing of Vaslet's picture by Mr. T. A. Dean, which appeared as the frontispiece to Tegg's edition of Wesley's *Natural Philosophy*. The original engraving is now very scarce.

The Portrait by Vaslet.

LIVING TO PLEASE GOD

THE generality of Christians, after using some prayer, usually apply themselves to the *business* of their calling. Every man that has any pretence to be a Christian will not fail to do this; seeing it is impossible that an idle man can be a good man,—sloth being inconsistent with religion. But with what view, for what end, do you undertake and follow your worldly business? 'To provide things necessary for myself and my family.' It is a good answer, as far as it goes; but it does not go far enough. For a Turk or a Heathen goes so far,—does his work for the very same ends. But a Christian may go abundantly farther. His end in all •his labour is to please God; to do, not his own will, but the will of Him that sent him into the world,—for this very purpose, to do the will of God on earth as angels do in heaven. He works for eternity. He 'labours not for the meat that perisheth' (this is the smallest part of his motive), 'but for that which endureth to everlasting life.' And is not this 'a more excellent way'?

Sermon on The More Excellent Way, *Works*, vii, 30.

XXIX.

The 'Nasmyth' Portrait

THIS engraving by N. Nasmyth is taken from a copperplate preserved at the Wesleyan Conference Office. It was published by R. Grant, Upper Thames Street, November 1791, a few months after Wesley's death.

The 'Nasmyth' Portrait.

CLAIMS OF A WIFE

THE person in your house that claims
your first and nearest attention, is, un-
doubtedly, your wife; seeing you are
to love her, even as Christ hath loved
the Church, when He laid down His life
for it, that He might 'purify it unto Himself, not having spot, or wrinkle, or any
such thing.' The same end is every
husband to pursue, in all his intercourse
with his wife; to use every possible
means that she may be freed from every
spot, and may walk unblamable in love.

Sermon, On Family Religion, *Works,*
vii. 78.

XXX.

The 'Aristocratic Wesley' Portrait

THIS portrait is in the possession of the Rev. Marmaduke Riggall. It impresses all who see it as a good painting. Dr. Watkinson calls it 'the Aristocratic Wesley.' 'The hair is iron-grey, the eye remarkably bright and full, the mouth sweet and firm.' The flesh-tint used makes Wesley appear stouter than he really was. It *may* have been engraved by Bromley for the *European Magazine,* April 1791.

The 'Aristocratic Wesley' Portrait.

THE CARE OF CHILDREN

NEXT to your wife are your children; immortal spirits whom God hath, for a time, entrusted to your care, that you may train them up in all holiness, and fit them for the enjoyment of God in eternity. This is a glorious and important trust; seeing one soul is of more value than all the world beside. Every child, therefore, you are to watch over with the utmost care, that, when you are called to give an account of each to the Father of Spirits, you may give your accounts with joy, and not with grief.

Sermon, On Family Religion, *Works*, vii. 79.

XXXI.

The Portrait by John Renton

THE Rev. W. G. Beardmore says of this portrait that 'no picture of Wesley has a greater air of reality and naturalness,' though 'in the somewhat heavy lower face it diverges from the majority of the Wesley portraits.' The engraving from which this reproduction is taken was executed and published by W. T. Fry in 1824. The career of Renton is somewhat obscure, though between 1799 and 1841 he exhibited many pictures (chiefly landscapes) at the principal art galleries. In the twenties of last century the names of Renton and Fry often appear together in the production of frontispiece portraits to the *Methodist Magazine*.

The Portrait by John Renton.

TRAINING THE YOUNG

YOUR children, while they are young, you may restrain from evil, not only by advice, persuasion, and reproof, but also by *correction;* only remembering that this means is to be used last,—not till all other have been tried, and found to be ineffectual. And even then you should take the utmost care to avoid the very appearance of passion. Whatever is done should be done with mildness; nay, indeed, with kindness too. Otherwise your own spirit will suffer loss, and the child will reap little advantage.

Sermon, On Family Religion, *Works,* vii. 80.

XXXII

The ' Hitt ' Portrait

THIS oil painting, according to a legend on the back, was given by Dr. Coke in 1808 to the Rev. Daniel Hitt, Methodist Book Agent in New York from 1808 to 1814. The original was destroyed by a fire in Cincinnati in 1868, where it had been sent to be lithographed, but Mr. Hitt's great-nephew sent to the Rev. J. Conder Nattrass a photograph of it which is here reproduced. The tradition was that Sir Joshua Reynolds was the painter, but of that there is no proof, and it has to be discredited (see also pp. 223 and 231).

The ' Hitt ' Portrait.

CHOICE OF A BUSINESS

WE may suppose that your sons have now been long enough at school, and you are thinking of some business for them. Before you determine anything on this head, see that your eye be single. Is it so? Is it your view to please God herein? It is well if you take Him into your account! But, surely, if you love or fear God yourself, this will be your first consideration,—' In what business will your son be most likely to love and serve God? In what employment will he have the greatest advantage for laying up treasure in heaven?' I have been shocked above measure in observing how little this is attended to, even by pious parents! Even these consider only how he may get most money; not how he may get most holiness! Even these, upon this glorious motive, send him to a heathen master, and into a family where there is not the very form, much less the power, of religion! Upon this motive they fix him in a business which will necessarily expose him to such temptations as will leave him not a probability, if a possibility, of serving God. O savage parents! unnatural, diabolical cruelty!—if you believe there is another world.

Sermon, On Family Religion, *Works*, vii. 84.

XXXIII.

The Portrait by Jackson .

THIS was painted in 1827 by John
Jackson, R.A. (1778-1831), at the
desire of an influential group of
Wesleyans, who wished to have a
standard typical portrait of Wesley.
Probably it is still the most familiar
of all Wesley's portraits, as for many
years it formed the frontispiece to
the Wesleyan Hymn-Book. Experts
differ greatly as to its value as a
faithful likeness, the general opinion
being that it is not a success in that
respect. The original is now at the
Wesleyan Book Room. Jackson was
a skilful artist, who also painted portraits of Benson, Fletcher, Watson,
and other early Methodist leaders.

The Portrait by Jackson.

SETTING GOD BEFORE OUR EYES

'BUT what shall I do?' Set God before your eyes, and do all things with a view to please Him. Then you will find a master, of whatever profession, that loves, or at least fears, God; and you will find a family wherein is the form of religion, if not the power also. Your son may nevertheless serve the devil if he will; but it is probable he will not. And do not regard, if he get less money, provided he get more holiness. It is enough, though he have less of earthly goods, if he secure the possession of heaven.

Sermon, On Family Religion, *Works*, vii. 85.

XXXIV.

The 'MacGowan' Portrait

THIS is by MacGowan, 1833, and is similar to that in the *European Magazine* (p. 159), reversed.

The 'MacGowan' Portrait.

VISITING THE SICK

How contrary to this is both the spirit and behaviour of even people of the highest rank in a neighbouring nation! In Paris, ladies of the first quality, yea, Princesses of the blood, of the Royal Family, constantly visit the sick, particularly the patients in the Grand Hospital. And they not only take care to relieve their wants (if they need anything more than is provided for them), but attend on their sick-beds, dress their sores, and perform the meanest offices for them. Here is a pattern for the English, poor or rich, mean or honourable! For many years we have abundantly copied after the follies of the French; let us for once copy after their wisdom and virtue, worthy the imitation of the whole Christian world. Let not the gentle-women, or even the Countesses, in England, be ashamed to imitate those Princesses of the blood! Here is a fashion that does honour to human nature. It began in France; but God forbid it should end there!

Sermon, On Visiting the Sick, *Works*, vii. 119.

XXXV.

The 'Mission House' Portrait

At the Wesleyan Mission House. It
is painted on glass, and described as
'the only original likeness as he
usually preached, aged 86, in John
Street Chapel, Spitalfields.' It hung
in the vestry there for many years
in the present frame, and was presented to Mr. Bestow by Phoebe
Francis, a very old Wesleyan, in
1846. It was put into a larger frame
for safety in 1858. The Rev. W. G.
Beardmore thought that it had
originally been painted on a window-
pane, and then removed. He regarded it as a unique and very
valuable portrait of Wesley.

The 'Mission House' Portrait.

CONSTANT COMMUNION

A SECOND reason why every Christian should do this as often as he can, is because the benefits of doing it are so great to all that do it in obedience to Him; viz., the forgiveness of our past sins, the present strengthening and re-freshing of our souls. In this world we are never free from temptations. Whatever way of life we are in, whatever our conditions be, whether we are sick or well, in trouble or at ease, the enemies of our souls are watching to lead us into sin. And too often they prevail over us. Now, when we are convinced of having sinned against God, what surer way have we of procuring pardon from Him than the 'showing forth the Lord's death'; and beseeching Him, for the sake of His Son's sufferings, to blot out all our sins?

Sermon on The Duty of Constant Communion, *Works,* vii. 148.

XXXVI.

The 'Ranmoor College' Portrait

THIS painting was until lately at Ranmoor College, Sheffield, and is now at Victoria Park United Methodist College, Manchester. It was presented to the Methodist New Connexion by James Wild, Esq., of Fulham House, near London, and described as 'a rare and valuable portrait of Mr. Wesley taken from life.' Mr. J. G. Wright, however, thought it might be a copy of the portrait by Hunter (see p. 90). We owe our information as to this portrait to the kindness of the Rev. Dr. George Eayrs.

The 'Ranmoor College' Portrait.

CONSTANTINE'S JOINING
CHURCH AND STATE

I HAVE been long convinced, from the whole tenor of ancient history, that this very event, Constantine's calling himself a Christian, and pouring that flood of wealth and honour on the Christian Church, the clergy in particular, was productive of more evil to the Church than all the ten persecutions put together. From the time that power, riches, and honour of all kinds were heaped upon the Christians, vice of all kinds came in like a flood, both on the clergy and laity. From the time that the Church and State, the kingdoms of Christ and of the world, were so strangely and unnaturally blended together, Christianity and Heathenism were so thoroughly incorporated with each other, that they will hardly ever be divided till Christ comes to reign upon earth. So that, instead of fancying that the glory of the New Jerusalem covered the earth at that period, we have terrible proof that it was then, and has ever since been, covered with the smoke of the bottomless pit.

Sermon, Of Former Times, *Works*, vii. 164.

XXXVII.

The 'Tomkinson-Dean' Portrait

Messrs. Tomkinson & Dean, of
Stoke-on-Trent, published this (litho-
graph portrait) in 1838. The drawing
was from a bust modelled from the
life by Enoch Wood of Burslem.
Mr. Wright thought it was the only
important portrait purporting to be
drawn from Wesley's bust. It is
accepted as a life-like presentation
of Wesley.

The 'Tomkinson-Dean' Portrait.

TENDERNESS OF CONSCIENCE

BUT sometimes this excellent quality, tenderness of conscience, is carried to an extreme. We find some who fear where no fear is; who are continually condemning themselves without cause; imagining some things to be sinful, which the Scripture nowhere condemns; and supposing other things to be their duty, which the Scripture nowhere enjoins. This is properly termed a scrupulous conscience, and is a sore evil. It is highly expedient to yield to it as little as possible; rather, it is a matter of earnest prayer that you may be delivered from this sore evil, and may recover a sound mind; to which nothing would contribute more than the converse of a pious and judicious friend.

Sermon, On Conscience, *Works,* vii. 191.

XXXVIII.

The ' Isaac Taylor ' Portrait

ISAAC TAYLOR used this portrait as
the frontispiece to his *Wesley and
Methodism* (1851). It has been attributed to Thomas Worlidge (1700-
1766), whose imitations of Rembrandt
are well known. When the portrait
came into Mr. Taylor's hands he was
told that it was taken from the side
gallery at the Foundery when Wesley
was preaching. W. Greatbach was
the engraver. Mr. Beardmore regarded it as 'a grotesque lampoon.'

The ' Isaac Taylor ' Portrait.

THE EVANGELICAL REVIVAL

THIS revival of religion has spread to such a degree as neither we nor our fathers had known. How *extensive* has it been! There is scarce a considerable town in the kingdom where some have not been made witnesses of it. It has spread to every age and sex, to most orders and degrees of men; and even to abundance of those who, in time past, were accounted monsters of wickedness.

Consider the *swiftness* as well as extent of it. In what age has such a number of sinners been recovered in so short a time from the error of their ways? When has true religion, I will not say since the Reformation, but since the time of Constantine the Great, made so large a progress in any nation, within so small a space? I believe hardly can either ancient or modern history afford a parallel instance.

Sermon, At the Foundation of City Road Chapel, *Works*, vii. 425.

XXXIX.

The 'Zobel' Portrait

THIS was engraved by George Zobel and published by William Tegg in 1866. It will be generally agreed that the face is too careworn and weary to be regarded as a good portrait.

The ' Zobel ' Portrait.

THE DEPTH OF THE REVIVAL

We may likewise observe the *depth* of the work so extensively and swiftly wrought. Multitudes have been thoroughly convinced of sin; and, shortly after, so filled with joy and love, that whether they were in the body, or out of the body, they could hardly tell; and, in the power of this love, they have trampled under foot whatever the world accounts either terrible or desirable, having evidenced, in the severest trials, an invariable and tender goodwill to mankind, and all the fruits of holiness. Now, so deep a repentance, so strong a faith, so fervent love, and so unblemished holiness, wrought in so many persons in so short a time, the world has not seen for many ages.

Sermon at the Foundation of City Road Chapel, *Works,* vii. 425.

XL.

The ' Forster ' Portrait

From the painting by the Canadian artist, Mr. J. W. L. Forster, who visited England in order to paint it after study of the Romney portrait. The original, with two others by the same artist—Charles and Susanna Wesley—hangs in Victoria College, Toronto; and a replica was given by the Methodists of Canada in 1922 to the Trustees of the Central Hall, Westminster.

The 'Forster' Portrait.

THE PURITY OF THE REVIVAL

No less remarkable is the *purity* of the religion which has extended itself so deeply and swiftly: I speak particularly as to the doctrines held by those who are the subjects of it. Those of the Church of England, at least, must acknowledge this; for where is there a body of people, who, number for number, so closely adhere to the doctrines of the Church?

Nor is their religion more pure from heresy than it is from *superstition*. In former times, wherever any unusual religious concern has appeared, there has sprung up with it a zeal for things that were no part of religion. But it has not been so in the present case; no stress has been laid on anything, as though it was necessary to salvation, but what is plainly contained in the word of God. And of the things contained therein, the stress laid on each has been in proportion to the nearness of its relation to what is there laid down as the sum of all,—the love of God and our neighbour. So pure, both from superstition and error, is the religion which has lately spread in this nation.

Sermon at the Foundation of City Road Chapel, *Works,* vii. 426.

XLI.

The 'Thursfield Smith' Portrait

THE painting from which this reproduction is taken belonged to Mr. R. Thursfield Smith, of Whitchurch. Both the artist and the origin of the picture are unknown. It represents Wesley in about middle life, but is unlike any other portrait of him. The size of the canvas is 28 by 23 ins. It was claimed to be the missing portrait by Sir Joshua Reynolds, but could not stand the test of critical examination.

The 'Thursfield Smith' Portrait.

OUTLOOK ON THE TIMES

WE see (and who does not?) the numberless follies and miseries of our fellow-creatures. We see, on every side, either men of no religion at all, or men of a lifeless, formal religion. We are grieved at the sight; and should greatly rejoice, if by any means we might convince some that there is a better religion to be attained,—a religion worthy of God that gave it. And this we conceive to be no other than love; the love of God and of all mankind; the loving God with all our heart, and soul, and strength, as having first loved *us,* as the fountain of all the good we have received, and of all we ever hope to enjoy; and the loving every soul which God hath made, every man on earth, as our own soul.

An Earnest Appeal, Works, viii. 3.

XLII.

The ' Rowell ' Portrait

THIS is from a crayon drawing of a painting once owned by Jacob Rowell, of Barnard Castle, who became one of Wesley's preachers in 1749. The portrait came into the possession of Mr. Anthony Steele of Barnard Castle.

The 'Rowell' Portrait.

A RELIGION FOR THE WORLD

THIS religion we long to see established in the world, a religion of love, and joy, and peace, having its seat in the inmost soul, but ever showing itself by its fruits, continually springing forth, not only in all innocence (for love worketh no ill to his neighbour), but likewise in every kind of beneficence, spreading virtue and happiness all around it.

An Earnest Appeal, Works, viii. 3.

XLIII.

The 'Castle' Portrait

FROM a painting attributed to Sir Joshua Reynolds. For fifty-seven years it belonged to a rector in Worcester, on whose decease it was bought by Mr. Jonathan Gates, a merchant in that city, who gave it forty-six years later to the Rev. John Webb, Congregational minister in Worcester. After his death Mr. W. Castle, of Forest Hill, secured it about 1891.

The 'Castle' Portrait.

ENTERING OPEN DOORS

THIS only we confess, that we preach
inward salvation, now attainable by faith.
And for preaching this (for no other
crime was then so much as pretended) we
were forbid to preach any more in those
churches, where, till then, we were gladly
received. This is a notorious fact. Being
thus hindered from preaching in the places
we should first have chosen, we now declare the 'grace of God which bringeth
salvation, in all places of His dominion';
as well knowing that God dwelleth not
only in temples made with hands. This
is the real, and it is the only real, ground
of complaint against us. And this we
avow before all mankind, we do preach
this salvation by faith. And not being
suffered to preach it in the usual places,
we declare it wherever a door is opened,
either on a mountain, or a plain, or by a
river side (for all which we conceive we
have sufficient precedent), or in prison,
or as it were, in the house of Justus, or
the school of one Tyrannus. Nor dare
we refrain. 'A dispensation of the Gospel
is committed to me; and woe is me, if I
preach not the Gospel.'

An Earnest Appeal, Works, viii. 28.

XLIV.

The 'Poxon' Portrait

THE original of this portrait was in 1910 in the possession of the trustees of the late Rev. John and Mrs. Poxon. It is in oils, and was presented to Mr. Poxon nearly seventy years ago by some wealthy friends. Mr. Poxon was a minister of the Methodist New Connexion, and died about the year 1890. In showing the portrait to his friends he always stated that it was an original painting of Wesley, executed after he was seventy years of age. The artist is unknown.

The 'Poxon' Portrait.

THE DAY OF THE LORD

BEHOLD, the day of the Lord is come! He is again visiting and redeeming His people. Having eyes, see ye not? Having ears, do ye not hear, neither understand with your hearts? At this hour the Lord is rolling away our reproach. Already His standard is set up. His Spirit is poured forth on the outcasts of men, and His love shed abroad in their hearts. Love of all mankind, meekness, gentleness, humbleness of mind, holy and heavenly affections, do take place of hate, anger, pride, revenge, and vile or vain affections. Hence, wherever the power of the Lord spreads, springs outward religion in all its forms. The houses of God are filled; the table of the Lord is thronged on every side. And those who thus show their love of God, show they love their neighbour also, by being careful to maintain good works, by doing all manner of good, as they have time, to all men. They are likewise careful to abstain from all evil. . . . All this is plain, demonstrable fact. For this also is not done in a corner. Now, do you acknowledge the day of your visitation? Do you bless God and rejoice therein?

An Earnest Appeal, Works, viii. 41.

XLV.

The 'Roberts' Portrait

Engraved by Roberts and published by Jaques and Wright, 13
Paternoster Row. Date unknown.

The 'Roberts' Portrait.

THE MARKS OF A METHODIST

'WHAT, then, is the mark? Who is a Methodist, according to your own account?' I answer: A Methodist is one who has 'the love of God shed abroad in his heart by the Holy Ghost given unto him'; one who 'loves the Lord his God with all his heart, and with all his soul, and with all his mind, and with all his strength.' God is the joy of his heart, and the desire of his soul; which is constantly crying out, 'Whom have I in heaven but Thee? and there is none upon earth that I desire beside Thee! My God and my all! Thou art the strength of my heart, and my portion for ever!'

The Character of a Methodist, Works, viii. 341.

XLVI.

The 'Russell' Portrait
at Kingswood

SAID to have been painted by John
Russell, R.A., in 1773. What has
been regarded as the original is in the
dining-hall at Kingswood School,
and a somewhat rough copy in Wesley's house at City Road. Mr.
Thursfield Smith, Mr. J. G. Wright,
and Rev. R. Green regarded the
former as Russell's work; but Dr.
G. C. Williamson, Russell's bio-
grapher, thinks it was either a con-
temporary copy of his picture, or a
very early copy of Bland's mezzotint
engraving (p. 98).

The 'Russell' Portrait at Kingswood.

THE RIGHT HAND OF FELLOWSHIP

Is thy heart right, as my heart is with thine? I ask no further question. If it be, give me thy hand. For opinions, or terms, let us not destroy the work of God. Dost thou love and serve God? It is enough. I give thee the right hand of fellowship. If there be any consolation in Christ, if any comfort of love, if any fellowship of the Spirit, if any bowels and mercies, let us strive together for the faith of the gospel; walking worthy of the vocation wherewith we are called; with all lowliness and meekness, with long-suffering, forbearing one another in love, endeavouring to keep the unity of the Spirit in the bond of peace; remembering there is one body and one Spirit, even as we are called with one hope of our calling; 'One Lord, one faith, one baptism; one God and Father of all, who is above all, and through all, and in you all.'

The Character of a Methodist, Works, viii. 347.

XLVII.

The Unfinished Portrait
after Russell

FROM a very rare unfinished mezzotint of the painting ascribed to
Russell, engraved by Jefferyes and
Faden. As may be seen, it was enclosed in a wide oval frame. The
copy has now been lost sight of.

The unfinished Portrait after Russell.

CHRISTIAN PERFECTION

By perfection I mean the humble, gentle, patient love of God, and our neighbour, ruling our tempers, words, and actions. I do not include an impossibility of falling from it, either in part or in whole.

As to the manner. I believe this perfection is always wrought in the soul by a simple act of faith; consequently, in an instant. But I believe a gradual work, both preceding and following that instant.

As to the time. I believe this instant generally is the instant of death, the moment before the soul leaves the body. But I believe it may be ten, twenty, or forty years before. I believe it is usually many years after justification; but that it may be within five years or five months after it, I know no conclusive argument to the contrary.

Christian Perfection, Works, xi. 446.

XLVIII.

The 'Enoch Wood' Bust

WESLEY gave five sittings for his bust to Mr. Enoch Wood in 1781, and told him he thought it much the best likeness that had been made of him. He, however, felt it had rather a melancholy expression. This was probably due to the fact that Wesley was generally engaged in writing during the sittings, and Mr. Wood drew his attention from his writing with some difficulty. He sat down again for a few minutes, and when the alteration was made, begged him not to touch it further lest he should mar it. This illustration is from one of the earliest examples, preserved in the Botteley Collection at the Wesleyan Conference Office, London.

The 'Enoch Wood' Bust.

VICTORY OVER RIOTERS

We came to Bolton about five in the
evening. We had no sooner entered the
main street than we perceived the lions at
Rochdale were lambs in comparison to
those at Bolton. Such rage and bitterness
I scarce ever saw before, in any creatures
that bore the form of men. They followed us in full cry to the house where
we went; and, as soon as we were gone
in, took possession of all the avenues to
it, and filled the street from one end to
the other. After some time the waves
did not roar quite so loud. . . . Believing
the time was now come, I walked down
into the thickest of them. They had
now filled all the rooms below. I called
for a chair. The winds were hushed,
and all was calm and still. My heart
was filled with love, my eyes with tears,
and my mouth with arguments. They
were amazed, they were ashamed, they
were melted down, they devoured every
word. What a turn was this! Oh, how
did God change the counsel of the old
Ahithophel into foolishness; and bring
all the drunkards, swearers, Sabbath-
breakers, and mere sinners in the place,
to hear of His plenteous redemption!

Journal, October 18, 1749.

XLIX.

The 'Roubiliac' Bust

THIS bust, which is of statuary marble and life-size, is in the National Portrait Gallery, London. It represents Wesley at about fifty or fifty-five, and is carefully wrought in all its details. It was reproduced in Parian ware about 1870 by Adams & Co., of Hanley (see *Wesleyan Methodist Magazine,* 1870). Many of Roubiliac's works (1695-1762) including the Nightingale Monument, are in Westminster Abbey.

The ' Roubiliac' Bust.

THE LAST PAGE OF THE JOURNAL

(LYNN) Tues. 19. In the evening all the clergymen in the town, except one who was lame, were present at the preaching. They are all prejudiced in favour of the Methodists; as indeed are most of the townsmen; who give a fair proof by contributing so much to our Sunday schools; so that there is near twenty pounds in hand.

Wed. 20. I had appointed to preach at Diss, a town near Scole; but the difficulty was, where I could preach. The minister was willing I should preach in the church, but feared offending the Bishop, who, going up to London, was within a few miles of the town. But a gentleman, asking the Bishop whether he had any objection to it, was answered, 'None at all.' I think this church is one of the largest in this county. I suppose it has not been so filled these hundred years. This evening and the next I preached at Bury, to a deeply attentive congregation, many of whom know in whom they have believed. So that here we have not lost all our labour.

Journal, October 19, 1790.

L.

The ' Adams-Acton ' Statue

THIS statue in front of City Road Chapel was unveiled by the Rev. W. F. Moulton, D.D., the President of the Conference, on March 2, 1891, the Centenary of Wesley's death. It is the work of Mr. Adams-Acton. The children of Methodism contributed the cost of £1,000. It stands on a base of polished Aberdeen granite. Wesley holds his famous 'Field' Bible in his hand, and underneath his feet is his great motto, 'The world is my parish.' Dean Farrar, then Canon and Archdeacon of Westminster, made a noble speech in Wesley's Chapel after the unveiling.

The 'Adams-Acton' Statue.

HIS LAST LETTER

(To William Wilberforce, M.P.)

LONDON, FEBRUARY 24, 1791.

MY DEAR SIR,

Unless the Divine Power has raised you up to be as Athanasius, *contra mundum*, I see not how you can go through your glorious enterprise in opposing that execrable villainy which is the scandal of religion, of England, and of human nature. Unless God has raised you up for this very thing, you will be worn out by the opposition of men and devils; but *if God be for you, who can be against you?* Are all of them together stronger than God? Oh, '*be not weary in well-doing.*' Go on, in the name of God and in the power of His might, till even American slavery, the vilest that ever saw the sun, shall vanish away before it. . . .

That He who has guided you from your youth up may continue to strengthen you in this and all things is the prayer of, dear sir, your affectionate servant,

JOHN WESLEY.

LI.

The 'Funeral Biscuit' Portrait

THIS portrait was engraved on an
envelope containing the 'funeral
biscuit' distributed to each of Wesley's friends at his funeral. Our reproduction is considerably enlarged
from the original. The lines around
the figure are from Young's 'Night
Thoughts' (Night II.).

The 'Funeral Biscuit' Portrait.

WESLEY'S DEATH-BED

JOSEPH BRADFORD, his old nurse, was with him. 'I have been reflecting on my past life,' the old man said to him: 'I have been wandering up and down between fifty and sixty years, endeavouring, in my poor way, to do a little good to my fellow-creatures; and now it is probable that there are but a few steps between me and death; and what have I to trust to for salvation? I can see nothing that I have done or suffered that will bear looking at. I have no other plea than this:

> I the chief of sinners am,
> But Jesus died for me.'

Moore, *Life of Wesley*, ii. 389.

The last word he was heard to articulate was 'Farewell!' 'Whilst (we) were kneeling around his bed, according to his often expressed desire, without a lingering groan, this man of God gathered up his feet in the presence of his brethren.'

Miss Ritchie's account of Wesley's death on March 2, 1791.

LII.

Portrait sketched by Ridley
after Wesley's Death

THIS portrait was drawn and engraved by William Ridley, who had a high reputation for careful work. It gives probably the most accurate outline of Wesley's features. It represents him as he lay in his coffin, and is very scarce. Its size is $7\frac{3}{4}$ by 6 inches.

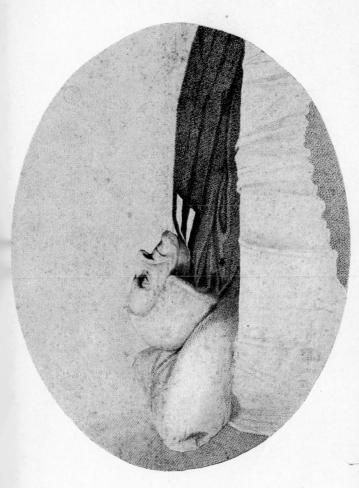

Portrait sketched by Ridley after Wesley's death.

267

PRINTED BY
RUSH & WARWICK,
HARPUR PRINTING WORKS,
BEDFORD.

DATE DUE

GAYLORD			PRINTED IN U.S.A.